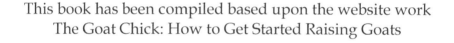

This book has been compiled based upon the website work
The Goat Chick: How to Get Started Raising Goats

The information and advice contained in this book should not
take the place of the advice of your goat veterinarian.

www.thegoatchick.com
The Goat Chick © 2017, 2018

ISBN-13: 978-1986181594
ISBN-10: 1986181596
1st Edition 032018

THE GOAT CHICK: HOW TO GET STARTED RAISING GOATS

Erica D. Hopkins

Illustrated by Ethan W. Fettig

Money can't buy happiness, but it can buy goats, and that's pretty much the same thing.

For Brandon

TABLE OF CONTENTS

#1 CHOOSE YOUR GOATS   10

Goat Myths Debunked   11
Goat Facts   13
Are Goats Really For Me?   15
Does, Bucks, or Wethers?   17
Which Breed is for Me?   20
Registered or Unregistered?   25
The Great Horn Debate   27
Selecting a Herd Size   29
Where Can I Find a Breeder?   31

#2 PREPARE FOR GOATS   34

What Kind of Housing Do Goats Need?   35
What Kind of Fencing Do Goats Need?   40
What Kind of Feed Should I Buy?   41
Which Tools & Supplies Do I Need?   42
How Do I Choose A Vet? A Mentor?   45

#3 WELCOME YOUR GOATS   46

Goat Anatomy   47
Goat Behavior   50
Assessing Goat Health   58
Diseases and Disorders   61
Medications   70
Controlling Parasites   75
FAMACHA   81
Toxic and Poisonous Plants   83
Feeding   84
Hoof Care   90
Grooming and Showing   92

Breeding   96
Planning Matings   105
Kidding   107
Kidding Issues (Dystocia)   115
Kid Care   124
Castrating   133
Horns, Scurs and Disbudding   136
Tattooing a Goat   139
Udders and Milking   142
Performance Programs   149
Understanding Pedigrees   151
Blue Eyed and Polled Genetics   157

AFTERWORD   161

#1

CHOOSE YOUR GOATS

This section is designed to give you general information about goats. It will help you decide if goats are right for you, and if so, which breed, herd size, sexes and characteristics you need to consider before starting your herd and your goat journey.

GOAT MYTHS DEBUNKED

There are many myths concerning goats. I've summarized the most popular ones here in the hopes that I can provide you with truthful information to help you decide whether you would like to become a goat owner.

#1 Goats Will Eat Anything
False. This myth was probably started because old cartoons depicted goats eating tin cans. Goats are vegetarians and are actually fairly picky about what they eat. If there was a tin can offered to them, they might mouth the paper label and even tear and eat the paper, but they do not, under any circumstances, eat tin cans.

#2 Goats Will Mow My Lawn For Me
Mostly False. Although goats do a great job of clearing brush from wooded areas, it is unlikely that they would keep your yard manicured enough to look "mowed." Goats are browsers, not grazers. They pick and choose what they want to eat and leave what they don't want to eat.

#3 All Goats Stink
False. Bucks (intact males) emit a strong odor that becomes worse during their breeding season known as "rut." Bucks also pee on their faces and all over everything else to attract females. Does (females) and wethers (castrated males) DO NOT STINK.

#4 Goats are Escape Artists
True AND False. Goats are curious creatures. Although it is true that some bratty goats just like to try to escape and get into trouble, for the most part, a goat who is happy with plenty enough to eat and drink are more likely to stay put where they are supposed to be...granted that all easy escape opportunities are minimized.

#5 If I Buy A Female Goat It Will Give Me Milk Forever
False. This is not really a myth, but I have answered this
question many, many times for people who did not know.
Like any other mammal, female goats must be bred and
freshen (have babies) to produce milk. A lactation, or the
period of time that a goat will produce milk, is typically 305
days, but that time can be longer or shorter based on various
factors. In short, a goat, generally, must be bred every year to
keep getting milk.

GOAT FACTS

- Goats are ruminants, which means that they have specialized four chamber stomachs in which they ferment and digest plant matter. Ruminants regurgitate partially digested food (cud) and chew it again to help the digestion process. Other ruminants include cattle, deer, sheep, and giraffe.

- Goats have horizontal pupils, which allow them to see behind them as predators approach. It is reported that their vision can cover up to 340 degrees! Because of the shape of their pupils, they also cannot look up or down without moving their heads, but they have excellent night vision.

- Due to the shape of the retina, goats do not have great depth perception, and are farsighted with a slight astigmatism.

- Goats do not have top teeth, only bottom teeth and extremely sharp molars where the action happens. Word to the wise: keep your fingers out the back of a goat's mouth!

- Goats do not have sweat glands, so they do not sweat. Instead they pant like dogs to cool themselves.

- Goats have been domesticated by humans for THOUSANDS of years!

- According to legend, coffee was discovered when an Ethiopian goat herder noticed his goats were jumping and dancing around after they ate coffee berries off bushes. THANKS GOATS!

- Goat milk is naturally homogenized, which means the cream does not readily rise to the top of the milk, like cow's milk.

- Many people who are lactose intolerant can drink goat milk because it contains less lactose, and the fat molecules are much smaller than cow's milk, making it easier for most people to digest.

ARE GOATS REALLY FOR ME?

There are many factors that you must consider before you start raising goats. The following questions are geared towards those who want goats for pets. If you decide to breed and milk, then there are ALOT more questions you need to ask yourself. These seven questions are a starting point. Answer them honestly to help you decide.

1. **First and foremost: Am I allowed to keep goats where I live?** If not, and you do it anyways, you are only asking for your goats to be seized and rehomed because you did not comply with your city/town regulations.

2. **Am I prepared to have at least two goats at all times?** Goats are herd animals. Generally, they do not do well if they live alone, as they can get very depressed and even die of loneliness. Goats must have another goat buddy to live and play with. Dogs, cats, horses, sheep, people and other livestock DO NOT COUNT. If one goat dies, you must buy another one, so that the survivor has a friend.

3. **Do I have enough space for goats?** At bare minimum, goats need a shelter that protects them from rain and wind, and an adequate fence to keep them where you want them. If left to roam, goats WILL EAT YOUR GARDEN, WANDER IN THE ROAD and COME IN YOUR HOUSE! You CAN dry lot goats (bring them all their food and water) but if they live in too small of a space you might compromise their health as they are prone to intestinal parasites. Access to pasture or fresh browse is highly recommended.

4. **Can I afford to feed my goats?** The cost of the goat itself is just the tip of the iceberg. If you do not have hay, then you must procure hay, which costs money. Goats cannot sustain life 365 days a year just eating your lawn. Goats need, at the very least, grass hay all day, every day to sustain life. What are you going to feed them in the winter when there is no grass, only snow? A pelleted grain is also recommended for growing animals and lactating does, as well as full-time access to a quality loose mineral.

5. **What will I do if my goat gets sick?** Do I have a mentor or a vet who I can consult when my goat gets sick? Do I have enough extra income to cover an emergency vet bill on Sunday, July 4th at 2am (TRUE STORY!)?

6. **Am I committed to providing care and maintenance to keep my goats happy and healthy?** In addition to food and water, goats need regular hoof care, vitamins and mineral supplements, and vaccinations (if you choose). Water buckets need constant attention, especially in the summer, when it needs changed out several times a day, and in the winter when the ice needs broken off the surface. Goat stalls and houses require regular maintenance to keep them clean enough to be a healthy environment.

7. **Do I have a person or persons who I can call to take care of my goats when I'm going to be out of town or away on vacation?** If not, you need to identify that person BEFORE you get goats.

Still want goats? Read on...

DOES, BUCKS OR WETHERS?

A female goat is called a doe. A male goat is called a buck, A castrated male goat is called a wether. Goat babies are called kids, or bucklings and doelings. Some people call goats Nannies and Billies, but these are slang terms, so you should get used to calling them by their correct terms if you want to be taken as a serious person who raises goats.

The sex of the goats you choose to raise is largely dependent upon what you want them for. This chart will help you decide what to get.

	COST	MAINTENANCE	HAS ODOR	CAN REPRODUCE	CAN GIVE MILK
DOES	$$$	HIGH	NO	YES	YES
BUCKS	$$	MID-LOW	YES	YES	NO
WETHERS	$	MID-LOW	NO	NO	NO
KIDS	$$$	HIGH	NO	YES	NO

Cost (to Purchase)- Does are the most expensive to buy because they can reproduce and give milk. Registered prices range from about $400 all the way up to several thousand dollars. You can expect to pay $100-$250 for unregistered stock. Bucks are generally about $100 cheaper than does, depending on what you get. Again, registered bucks can range from around $300 all the way up to several thousand dollars. Kid prices are comparable to registered doe and buck prices depending on their pedigrees. Wethers cost $50 on the low end, up to around $200 on the high end.

At my farm, Twin Willows, I use a sliding scale to price registered animals. The base price is $450 and it goes up from there based on accomplishments of the animal itself and her parents. I sell wethers for $150 each.

Maintenance- Wethers require the least maintenance, followed by bucks. The general maintenance of wethers is limited based on the fact that they are not breeding animals. Breeding animals require more maintenance than wethers, with kids requiring the most maintenance, especially if they are not yet weaned.

Odor- Bucks (and young bucks over 4-ish months old) pee on their faces, on the backs of their legs, on their beards, and really...everywhere. The urine obviously has an odor and it smells stronger during their breeding season (rut). Wethers do not stink. Does do not stink. Kids do not stink.

Reproducing- Does and Bucks can reproduce. Doelings (doe kids) as young as 5ish months, and Bucklings (buck kids) as young as seven weeks CAN REPRODUCE, though not suggested. Wethers cannot reproduce, as long as BOTH testicles have been completely removed. Wethers can live with bucks, does, and other wethers. Does of some goat breeds come into season (heat) every month, so it is not suggested that bucks of any age be housed with does. Goat gestation is 150 days for standard breeds and 145 days for miniature breeds. Does can have ONE to SEVEN (Guiness World Record Pending) babies in a litter.

Can Give Milk- Does will lactate if they are bred and will produce milk after they freshen (give birth). In general, a lactation lasts 305 days. Does can lactate shorter or longer than 305 days based on several factors, including their food intake and how their udders are maintained. We will talk more about kidding and milking later.

In Summation: Does and wethers make great pets. Depending on your reasons for keeping goats, you can use the chart on the previous pages to help you make decisions. Bucks are not horrible creatures. In fact, all of the bucks at my farm are very friendly. However, bucks should only be kept for breeding purposes because of the separate housing requirements and the annoying smell. Obviously, if your intention is to breed, you are going to need a buck or access to a buck to service your doe(s). We will delve further into that later.

Still want goats? Let's explore the breeds...

WHICH BREED IS FOR ME?

There are many choices for you when it comes to choosing a breed of goat. In the United States, goats are basically classified into three different categories: Dairy, Meat, and Fiber. You should choose the category and breed that works best for you for your purposes.

Dairy Goats

Dairy Goats are bred for milk, so we will focus on the dairy goat's purpose which is...MILK! These numbers were compiled from the ADGA 2016 Knowledgebase and ADGA & AGS Breed Standards. Note: One gallon of milk weighs approximately 8 lbs.

	Average BodyWt Adult Doe	Height at Withers (Doe)	Average Daily Production (in lbs)	Average Milk Fat %
Alpine	135 lbs+	> 30 inches	8.5 lbs	3.3%
Lamancha	130 lbs+	> 28 inches	7.4 lbs	3.7%
Nigerian Dwarf	75 lbs	<22.5 inches	2.4 lbs	6.4%
Nubian	135 lbs+	> 30 inches	6.5 lbs	4.7%
Oberhasli	120 lbs +	> 28 inches	7.3 lbs	3.8%
Saanan	135 lbs+	> 30 inches	9.1 lbs	3.3%
Sable Saanan	135 lbs+	> 30 inches	7.6 lbs	3.3%
Toggenburg	120 lbs+	> 26 inches	7.2 lbs	3.2%

As you can see, there are tradeoffs to every breed of dairy goat. The bigger the breed, the more they eat. Standard breeds produce more milk but have a lower fat content. The Nigerian is compact, eats much less than a standard goat and has the highest butterfat, which will produce a sweeter milk and the best yield if you will be making products such as cheese, yogurt and kefir. I admit that I am biased and chose the Nigerian Dwarf for their small size and the quality of their milk.

You choose what's best for you.   Also, please remember that if you choose to have milk, you MUST breed the doe in order for her to lactate. Dairy wethers make perfect pets and of course, they cannot breed, so you don't have to worry about breeding and milking.

Meat Goats

Meat goats are bred for meat. In general, meat goats have more muscle mass than dairy goats due to their purpose, which is meat.

Despite being classified as red meat, goat is leaner and contains less cholesterol, fat, and protein than both lamb and beef, and less energy than beef or chicken; therefore, it requires low-heat, slow cooking to preserve tenderness and moisture.

Below are some breeds you may want to consider if you would like to breed meat goats:

Boer- The Boer goat is a South African meat goat with a large frame. They are white and reddish-brown, or all red, short-haired, and with black, brown or red markings on the head and neck.

Spanish- Before Boer goats became available in the US in the late 1980s, Spanish goats were the standard meat goat breed, especially in the South. These goats are descendants of goats brought by Spanish explorers. They're medium-sized and lanky, mostly short-haired, and come in all colors.

Myotonic (Fainting)- Developed in Tennessee, these goats go rigid and "faint" or fall down when startled. Myotonic goats are hardy, fertile, and have a long breeding season.

Kiko- Large-framed, white, hardy and able to thrive under poor conditions, the Kiko was developed in New Zealand and brought to the US in the 1990s. Kikos are strictly meat producing goats.

Pygmy- Pygmy goats are mostly pets, but they do have some potential for meat because they have a compact and meaty body and are fertile out of season. Pygmies are often mistaken for Nigerian Dwarves and vice versa. However, they are two separate breeds.

Hair and Fiber Goats

Angora

Angoras have long, wavy coats, with fiber called mohair. They are usually white. They have short, curved horns, which are usually left on the goat, because they may regulate body temperature. The average adult goat produces 8 to 16 pounds of mohair each year, while kids give from 3 to 5 pounds of longer, finer hair.

Cashmere

Cashmere goats in the United States aren't a breed but a type of goat. Feral goats from Australia and Spanish goats in the United States are both cashmere producers. Cashmere goats are dual fiber/meat goats.

Pygora

The Pygora is a cross between the Pygmy and the Angora. The Pygora is a small, easy-to-handle, and good-tempered fiber goat.

Nigora

Nigoras are a cross between a Nigerian Dwarf and an Angora. They have the advantage of producing colorful fiber as well as milk.

In Conclusion: There are many types and breeds of goats. Be aware that there are also many, many crossbreeds (or grades) that can result in goats with an endless array of characteristics. Choosing the type and breed of goat that you want to raise is highly dependent on what you want them for.

REGISTERED OR UNREGISTERED?

Many registries exist to keep pedigrees and record births. For dairy goats, there is the American Dairy Goat Association, and the American Goat Society, as well as many specific breed registries. There are also registries for miniature goats, meat goats, and fiber goats. There are many beautiful, healthy goats who are not registered out there, but there are some distinct advantages to having registered goats.

Since the entire point of breeding goats is (or should be) to improve the breed, the most obvious advantage of raising registered goats is that you can track the animal's ancestry and thus, it's genetic history.

All registries require a fee to be paid to them in order for them to manage your pedigrees, which is usually higher for non-members of the organization. Registered animals have an official registered name, and are most often identified by tattoos in their ears or on their tails, which identify them from every other goat in the registry. Registries keep track of pedigrees, show wins, appraisal scores, production (milk) data, and other important DNA and genetic data used by breeders to improve their goats towards the ideal animal.

Because of the work that goes into, and comes out of registered stock, you can expect to pay more for them than unregistered stock. Relatedly, you can also expect to get more profit out of registered stock when you sell them or sell the registered babies from them. There are rules to which animals can be and can't be registered. In the case of Nigerian Dwarfs, an animal can only be registered if both parents were registered because their herd book is closed, rather than open.

A word of caution: Just because an animal is "registered" does not mean that it is "good", and it also doesn't mean that it's healthy and disease free. We will talk more about that later.

THE GREAT HORN DEBATE

Most breeders are very passionate about this topic to one side or the other. I don't care either way if you decide to keep horned goats, or if you keep disbudded or polled (naturally hornless) animals. In some breeds, horns are encouraged including many of the meat and fiber breeds. I raise dairy goats. The only thing I can tell you is why I choose to raise goats without horns.

Registered dairy goats cannot have horns. If they are not polled, then they must be disbudded shortly after birth. Hornless goats are safer. There are no worries about them hurting others with them or getting their horns stuck in the fence and hanging themselves. I will not knowingly sell a disbudded goat into a herd with horned goats. The risk of injury is too great, and I have put too much work into my babies just to have them gored. Should you decide to have horned goats, you should be prepared for the consequences of having them.

But, just as importantly, should you decide to have goats disbudded at birth, you either must learn how to do it yourself or have an experienced person or veterinarian do it for you. In six years of breeding, I have never learned, nor have I ever wanted to learn, how to do it. Disbudding, or burning the horn buds with a hot iron, is the safest and most humane method of removing horns. Disbudding paste SEEMS more humane, but I promise you, it is not! Disbudding with paste causes WEEKS of pain for the baby, as opposed to just a few minutes of pain from the hot iron. My husband disbuds all goats born on the farm in the first few days of life. At those times, I run far, far away because I just can't stand the smell of burning hair. The good news is that, if done correctly, the iron is only on their heads for a few seconds, and babies recover almost instantly. We will talk more about disbudding later.

You might be thinking right now...well I'll just buy polled (naturally hornless) goats. Good thought, but that's not how it works. Breeding a polled goat to a horned goat still almost always results in some horned babies. Breeding a polled goat to a polled goat is NEVER ADVISED because of the increased risk of hermaphroditic offspring. It's okay to have a few polled goats around, but it's simply impossible to get around having babies born with horn buds if you are breeding.

Still want goats? You sure? Read on.

SELECTING A HERD SIZE

So, if you've read this far, you are probably still serious about getting goats, but how many should you get? For this section, I've developed a system of herd classification that I will refer to several times in future sections. Let's define them.

Level 1 Herd: Backyard Goats
The Level 1 herd consists of 2+ animals that are strictly kept for pets. Most often, this herd is made up of several wethers or does and wethers. If a doe resides in the herd, she is never bred. They live in small shelters or sheds in backyards, so they might also be referred to as "Backyard Goats."

If you want a Level 1 Herd, start with two wethers.

Level 2 Herd: Milk Production
The Level 2 herd consists of a small group of does that are serviced by one buck, either on the property or from another breeder, to bring them into their lactations. This herd is kept strictly for milk production purposes. Milk is used by the family for drinking, to make cheese and other dairy products, or to produce soaps and lotions. Babies born from the breedings are quickly sold at birth or at weaning, most often as pets.

If you want a Level 2 Herd, start with two does and a wether. Later, you can bring in a buck to service your does and move the wether to bunk with him when he is not "working". If you choose a breed that enters estrus all year (like Nigerian Dwarf, Pygmy, Myotonic) does can be bred at the same time to milk seasonally, or their breedings can be staggered to keep at least one doe in milk at all times.

Level 3 Herd: Goat Breeder

The Level 3 herd consists of any number of does and bucks who are kept specifically for breeding and improving the herd they reside within. Breedings are carefully orchestrated. Most babies born from breedings are probably sold, but are carefully scrutinized before offering for sale or kept for further use within the herd. Level 3 herds cull their animals often to weed out those who do not conform to what they want, and many times bring in better animals to improve specific traits within their herds.

If you want a Level 3 Herd, there is really only one rule for selecting animals. Buy the best conformed does and bucks that you can afford. Doing so will go a long way towards getting to your goals, because the closer you are to what you want, the sooner it comes. Many people do not realize that from the time a "keeper" doe is born, until the time you can determine if you want her to remain in the herd can take 2.5-3.5 years! That is ALOT of time to invest in one animal if you are wrong about her!

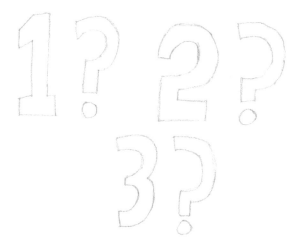

Still want goats? Let's talk about where to find them!

WHERE CAN I FIND A BREEDER?

No matter which herd level you decide upon, you should ALWAYS buy goats from a reputable breeder who has PROOF that the animal you are buying is free from CAE. Caprine Arthritis Encephalitis (CAE) is a debilitating, deadly disease that is reportedly present in over 80% of herds in the United States. You do not want this disease in your herd. We will learn more about infectious diseases in later segments. For now, you only need to know that you are buying from a regularly tested herd before you go any further.

CAUTION: DO NOT BUY ANIMALS FROM THE SALE BARN! Why do you think they are there? Sale barn animals are good for one thing...slaughter. I can't tell you how many times someone has called me asking for help with their goat they just bought from the sale barn yesterday, and it is dying today. Just DON'T DO IT!

Some tips for finding a breeder:
- A quick Google search in your state will bring up many choices for the breed you select.
- Visit some farms that raise the breed you choose to get an idea of what it takes to get started.
- You can also use www.goatfinder.com to find breeders of your chosen breed.
- Facebook has recently made live animal sales on the site, illegal. There are still reputable breeders there selling their animals, you just have to look harder to find them.
- Some breeders use Craigslist to move animals. Search for goats available in your area.
- Join goat groups on the internet or on Facebook and ask for recommendations for breeders.

Where ever you choose to buy your goats from, remember to always ask for a negative CAE test dated within the last year, or if the animal is less than 1 year of age, ask for negative CAE test results from both parents. The test report will state the animals name and/or tattoo or tag identifier and will give result as NEGATIVE or POSITIVE.

Also, you want to make sure that you receive a copy of and understand a breeder's sales policy. Most breeders post their sales policies on their website. If they do not have one posted, ask them. Some breeders charge a reservation fee while other offer free reservations to reserve an animal out of a particular breeding. Make sure you understand if your deposit is non-refundable or is transferable to other animals, and how long you have to pick up your animals. You might need to arrange transport either by air or ground transport. Failure to understand the sales policies of your chosen breeder can cost you money in boarding fees if the animal is not picked up by the deadline.

Breed(s) I want to raise: _____

Herk Level:

___ Backyard Goats (Pets)
___ Milk Production
___ Goat Breeder

Notes:

#2
PREPARE FOR GOATS

By now, I hope you have chosen your breed of goats and a herd size that will work for you. If you haven't chosen yet, that's OKAY! I hope this section will bring you closer to your decision. We will now explore important subjects as housing, fencing, and feeding, to help you along on your goat journey.

WHAT KIND OF HOUSING DO GOATS NEED?

As I mentioned in the previous section, goats need, at a bare minimum, a shelter that protects them from wind and rain. Although they are very hardy and adapt to most climates, most goats hate rain, mud, and snow, so you will need a sturdy structure for them to live in. The elaborence of the structure can be left up to interpretation, but should suit the needs for what you are raising goats for. For this discussion we will break it down by Herd Levels. We will talk more about exactly which supplies you need later, but for now this will provide a general overview.

First, some information about temperature. My goats live in an insulated barn equipped with a wood stove. They do not need to live in a heated barn, but it's nice to be able to take the edge off in the winter and provide heat for the babies when they are born. That being said, most goats can live in extreme temperatures, provided that they can stay dry, and they have adequate food, water and minerals.

Level One Herd (Backyard Goats)
Two goats can absolutely live in a large dog house, calf hut, or small shed, but before you go out and buy these things, let's consider some other things. Even if you are keeping goats for pets, you are still going to need storage space for hay, feed, medications, and other maintenance supplies. If you have somewhere else to store these things, then a dog house or small shed would be fine. If you do not have the storage for hay and equipment then perhaps you should provide your goats a small shed with a hay loft with enough room for a cabinet full of supplies and medications. It is also recommended that you invest in a small stanchion (goat stand) so that you can lock down your goats while you provide them hoof care and administer vitamins and medication. Be sure that you have a place for that as well.

Level Two Herd (Milk Production)

Breeding even a few goats once per year requires more space for storage of essential items than a Level One Herd. Remember that you will be breeding, kidding and milking, so you need separate dedicated spaces for those events. A medium sized shed or space dedicated in a larger barn will work perfectly for the situation.

Things to keep in mind: You will need a space for the does to kid. It does not need to be elaborate, and it can be as simple as a temporary 5X5 metal wire pen, but it should provide privacy and separation from your other does, as most does who have just kidded get a little "testy" if other does approach their newborns. They eventually get over their protectiveness as the hormones start to wane from their bodies a few days after kidding. A source of heat is highly recommended so electric should be available in the kidding stalls. I usually keep heat on my babies from kidding until the babies are approximately 2 weeks old. The safest source of direct heat is the Premiere One Prima Heat Lamps although I do admit that I had one catch fire once due to a malfunction. For the most part, these are the safest choice. Never use a heat lamp without a housing guard. Another good heat source that I have recently found is the Sweeter Heater which is a safe source of radiant heat which can be used to provide heat for newborns in cold weather.

You will need a space to milk the does. You should buy or make a stanchion and position it in a room that you can keep very clean. Most farms that breed goats construct a milk parlor that doubles as a maintenance room, but keep in mind that milking a couple of does does not necessarily require a dedicated milk parlor. You can station the stanchion under a covered porch to milk out your does. Just be aware that when it is -20° F, those does are still going to need to be milked, and you will also be exposed to the elements as you work.

If you will be housing a buck, even temporarily, he will need a separate enclosure and fence to live within while he is not working. You might also need separate housing for baby bucks and does who are weaned and waiting for their new homes.

You will also need a space for hay, feed and maintenance supplies, just as you would with a Level One herd. I find it easiest to build my maintenance station into my milk parlor, because all of my supplies are right next to the stanchion, should I need them.

Level Three Herd: Goat Breeder
This level requires all of the supplies required of a Level Two Herd, with some optional additions. I have a Level Three Herd, where I carefully orchestrate breedings, plan for kiddings, and scrutinize babies that are born to determine whether they will join the herd. There is nothing to say that you can't be a serious breeder with a Level Two Herd setup, but if you want your setup to work FOR you and not AGAINST you, there are some things you need to consider.

BEFORE you start building, let me advise a word of caution: Whatever you build, DO NOT build anything TOO permanent. Throwing up panels for a makeshift pen is easy. Tearing down walls when you decide it doesn't work is much more difficult. Layout your barn with your best guess on what will work, and then use it for awhile. After some time, you will figure out ways to make your layout work better for you and THEN once you have worked within your setup and have decided on a final layout, you can build it permanently.

If you are a Level Three Herd, you will most likely have at least one buck (and a wether for a buddy), several senior does, yearling dry does, and a gaggle of babies at some point in the year. Doelings and bucklings should be housed separately after the bucklings reach seven weeks of age, if not at birth. Not only do they need separate pens, but they need to be babyproofed pens as well. Where will you put a goat that is sick and needs to be separated from the herd? Think about where you are going to put everyone when your herd is at maximum capacity and everything has gone wrong.

My herd usually consists of 50+ animals in the spring. I have a general population pen with 24/7 pasture access to three acres for the junior and senior does. I have a separate pen and three acre pasture for the junior and senior bucks on the other side of the barn. I have a large indoor pen that I can open up to the gen pop pen for extra indoor space, or I can use it to house junior bucks before they are banded or those senior does who need a little extra feed to keep weight on them.

I also have three separate kidding stalls and I have at times added 5 x 5 metal wire pens to my milk parlor when I run out of kidding stalls in the spring. When I am not kidding, I can use the kidding stalls to quarantine sick or newly acquired goats. My setup works very well, but it is still not ideal. I would like to have a separate yard for the large inside pen. I would like to have more kidding stalls. I would like to have another separate area for bucklings, and one for doelings, and one for yearling dry does, and another for skinny does who need more food. All with separate pastures, of course. I would like to have the space to rotate pastures so that I can let one pasture rest while they graze on the other. I will probably never have the ultimate setup unless I build another barn and acquire more property. After I win the lottery, of course. But like I said...what I have works, and I'm pretty content with that. It also makes it very nice to have water and electricity to the barn. That water spigot 50 feet away from your barn might not seem like a big deal now, but once you are carrying five gallon buckets in a foot of snow when it's below zero day after day, you might change your tune. Luckily, teeing into an outside waterline at the spigot is fairly easy, and can be completed in a weekend. My next task in my barn is to add an on-demand water heater. They are relatively inexpensive and will save me from trekking to the house when I need hot water. It might seem petty but when you spend hours per day in a barn tending to your animals, it's those little creature comforts that make the difference between dreading or loving your time in the barn.

WHAT KIND OF FENCING DO GOATS NEED?

Fencing serves two purposes: keeping animals in and keeping predators out. That being said, no matter which kind of fencing you choose, I truly believe that installing an electric fence (hot wire) is important to all Herd Levels. Depending on your setup, you might choose to hot wire the perimeter of your property, to keep coyotes and neighborhood dogs far away from your goats, and then use regular cattle panel or 2X4 welded wire fencing for your actual pen enclosures. I would advise against using cattle panel anywhere on your farm if you are going to be raising horned goats, as their heads can get easily stuck. Welded wire fencing is best for horned goats. You can also use electric tape or portable solar electric net fencing from Premier 1 and move your fencing around to different areas at your leisure.

Welded wire fencing (2X4) works very well to keep both babies and adult in. Cattle and hog panels work well in adult enclosures, but babies can usually get through. If you do decide to use cattle or hog panels, make sure you reinforce the bottom 12-24 inches with chicken wire or 2 X 4 welded wire fencing in areas in which babies will be kept. As for posts, you can use regular metal fence posts, wooden posts, or even step-in posts in some cases. We have a side pasture that we sometimes let the bucks into, which consists of step-ins placed 8 feet apart, and two hot wires strategically placed so that they can't go over, under or through. It works well most of the time, but every once in awhile you will get a goat that figures out how to shimmy his way through or jump over, and then proceeds to teach the others how to get out. Because of this reason, I would only suggest using this setup on a temporary basis and not as a permanent fencing option.

WHAT KIND OF FEED SHOULD I BUY?

We will talk extensively about feed in the next section "Welcome Your Goats," but here in an overview:

A goat's main diet is hay. At least grass hay or pasture should be available to goats at all times. Alfalfa or a similar legume hay is best for pregnant and lactating does as it provides more protein and calcium for growing babies and producing milk. The nutritional content of the hay is more important than the kind of hay you choose to feed. All hay should be analyzed for protein content and ADF (acid detergent fiber), which is the indigestible part of hay. More on that later.

In addition to hay, a high-quality grain with at least 16% protein content should be fed to pregnant does, lactating does and growing babies. Sweet Feed does not usually provide enough protein. Use a pelleted grain, whole grain, textured grain or rolled grain instead. Be careful not to surpass the recommended serving size for the animal's weight located on the bag. Any increase in feed rations should be done slowly, because changes in feed can throw off the animal's digestive balance and can make her very, very sick.

Goats also need balanced vitamins and minerals in their diet which is administered to them via their hay, their feed, loose minerals and supplements. To determine the correct balance of feed for your goats, read on.

WHICH TOOLS AND SUPPLIES DO I NEED?

The handy list on following two pages will provide you with all the necessary supplies for your chosen herd level. For an explanation of herd levels, revisit the last section, Choose Your Goats.

All items which are marked with an **X** are highly recommended.

	LEVEL 1	LEVEL 2&3
General Care & Maintenance	HERD	HERDS
Stanchion (Goat Stand)	X	X
Hoof Shears and Hoof Pick	X	X
Grooming Brush	X	X
Collars and Leashes	X	X
Hay Feeder, Feed Pans and Water Buckets	X	X
Loose Mineral Feeder	X	X
First Aid/Medical		
Epinephrine (Rx Only)	X	X
Thermometer	X	X
Animal Scale or Weight Tape	X	X
Small Drench Syringes	X	X
Blood Stop Powder	X	X
NutriDrench	X	X
Baking Soda	X	X
Mineral Oil (for bloat)	X	X
3cc Syringes and 20 Gauge Needles	X	X
Broad Spectrum Antibiotic (Pen G)	X	X
ProBios Paste	X	X
Vitamin B Complex	X	X
Fir Meadows Gut Soothe	X	X
Activated Charcoal	X	X
Lactated Ringers (IV Saline Fluid)	X	X
Banamine (Rx Only)	X	X
CD&T Vaccine (if you choose to vaccinate)	X	X
Tetanus Antitoxin	X	X
C&D Antitoxin	X	X
BoviSera	X	X
DiMethox	X	X
SMZ-TMP	X	X
Ivomec Injectible 1%	X	X
Cydectin Pour-On Cattle Dewormer	X	X
Ivermectin Dewormer		X
BoSe (Rx Only)	X	X
Copper Bolus	X	X
Lutalyse (Rx Only)		X
Oxytocin (Rx Only)		X

Advanced Supplies for Level 2 & 3 Herds Only

Kidding & Kid Supplies
Surgical Gloves & Lubricant
Absorbent Pads & Towels
Bulb Aspirator
Iodine & Surgical Scissors
Insulin Syringes
Feeding Tube & Large Slip Syringe
Baby Enema (6cc Slip Syringe & IV tubing)
Kids Coats or Sweaters
Pritchard Nipples and Empty Soda Bottles
Tattoo Outfit with Green Paste Ink
Disbudding Iron & Disbudding Box
Elastrator and Castrating Bands

Milking Supplies
Teat Wash (5% Bleach Water/Baby Wipes)
Teat Dip or Teat Spray (FightBac)
Stainless Milking Pail
Milk Strainer, Filter or Cheesecloth
Mastitis Testing Kit

HOW DO I CHOOSE A VET?
HOW DO I FIND A MENTOR?

Getting help from the experts is important, especially in an emergency situation. It's best to be as prepared as possible before an emergency happens, so it's extremely important that you have both a veterinarian and a goat mentor on speed dial. Finding a veterinarian in some areas can be challenging, so find a goat breeder in your area first and ask for a recommendation for a veterinarian who is experienced with goats.

Many breeders who live in places where goat veterinarians are sparce tend to do most of their own veterinary medicine for their herds, but build a relationship with a large animal vet who is willing to provide prescriptions and emergency care, when needed. Point blank...you need a vet to call in an emergency (Kidding Problems, C-sections, Major Injuries, etc) and that number should be posted in a primary location so that you can find it quickly. For less than immediate emergencies, you should have an experienced goat breeder you can call and is willing to answer questions and provide advise. There are many goat community groups on the internet and on social media sites that you can explore to try to find a goat mentor.

#3
WELCOME YOUR GOATS

In this section, we will learn more about how to care for your goats, how to make sure they stay healthy, and how to deal with problems that arise along your goat journey.

GOAT ANATOMY

External Parts of the Goat

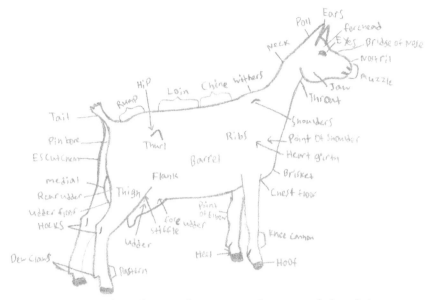

The above graphic shows the external parts of the dairy goat. It is important that you learn the basic external parts of the goat so that not only you can relay information, but also so that you understand the underpinnings of breed conformation characteristics. Generally, the better conformed (conforms to breed standards) a goat, the more productive life you will get out of the animal. This is especially important for breeders, for those who participate in goat shows and production programs, and for those who are producing products (i.e. milk) from the animals.

We will not talk about goat conformation here, but you can find more information about this subject from your breed registry.

Digestive System of the Ruminant

Goats are ruminants, which means they have highly specialized four chamber stomachs to digest food. The following is a crude explanation of how food is digested.

Food (plant matter) is chewed and swallowed by the goat and it first enters the rumen where it is partially digested. As the food digests, it is layered into solid and liquid matter. The solid matter in the rumen then travels to the reticulum where it is regurgitated (cud) so that the goat can mix the undigested solids with saliva. Goats chew their cud on a regular basis and when they swallow it again, the cud enters the omasum for further processing. The food in the omasum then moves to the abomasum and onto the small and large intestines and out through the anus. At the same time, liquids are processed into urine and exit through the urethra. Goat poop exits as round, hard, rather dry little pellets, very similar to rabbit pellets.

Goat Teeth

The teeth of the goat are worth mentioning, because they are interesting and unique. Goats do not have teeth in their upper jaw, only their lower. Their upper lips are highly animated, and are used to grab and pull foliage off of trees and weeds. They have a smooth dental pad in the tops of their mouths, and also sharp molars in the back of their mouths on the top and bottom jaws which are used to shred sticks and twigs.

Kids are usually born with teeth or with at least the emergence of teeth. Their first teeth are called milk teeth. You will probably never see a lost goat tooth in the goat yard, but they do, in fact, lose their baby teeth, which are replaced with full adult teeth in their fifth year.

Doe (Female) Reproductive System

Some goats, including miniature and meat breeds, can breed year-round. Most standard breeds come into estrus (heat) in the late summer, fall and early winter. The estrus cycle of the goat is approximately every 21 days. A doe is in estrus for approximately 30 hours. She has two ovaries from which she releases eggs and hormones, and also has a divided uterus with a right and left horn. Standard breeds generally have one to three babies at a time, with quadruplets being rare. Minis can have one to four babies, with quintuplets being rare. The current world record (pending) for number of babies in a single goat (Nigerian Dwarf) birth is SEVEN.

Buck (Male) Reproductive System

The intact buck has two large testicles between it's legs which produce semen to impregnate does. When the testicles are removed either by banding, or by surgical procedure, the buck can no longer reproduce. A castrated buck is called a wether. More on castrating later.

The penis of the mature buck is sheathed inside the body. Bucklings cannot extend their penis until they hit puberty. The penis extends outside the body for reproduction and when the buck is excited and urinating. The penis is extremely long and can extend far forward towards the front legs. Bucks regularly urinate on the backs of their legs and on their beards and in their mouths when they are excited. They do this to create the bucky stench that does go crazy for.

GOAT BEHAVIOR

I bought my first two Nigerian Dwarf goats back in May of 2011. It took me all of two seconds to fall head over heels in love with them. Since then, I have watched my goats for thousands of hours. Some of the information below provides general information on goat behaviors, and others are a synopsis of what I have observed in my own herd. Goats are friendly, smart and interesting creatures and it's important to know what to expect when you decide to keep goats.

The Flehmen Response

The Flehmen Response is evident when the goat curls his or her upper lip, stretches the neck and looks like he is sniffing the air with his lips. Both male and female goats of any age can exhibit this response. Also, many other animals exhibit the Flehmen Response including horses, giraffe, donkeys, cats, yak, cows, sheep and even rhinos.

The response is triggered when the goat smells something and must investigate further. Goats, and all animals who show the Flehmen, have an olfactory sensory organ on the roof of their mouths, called the Jacobson's organ, where they can "smell" and sense pheromones. The reason for the Flehmen Response is simply self-communication. Goats will use the Flehmen when they smell something they are interested in and use it to gather information about the smell. Urine, feces and birthing fluids are often investigated with the Flehmen, as well as a doe's hind end to check for stage of estrus. The results of their investigation provides the goat an answer to "What's that smell?" We will talk more about the Flehmen Response in the next section.

Fun Fact: Flehmen means "to bare the upper teeth" in German.

"Pawing" the Ground

Yes, I know. Goats don't have paws. I'm using this term as a verb. =)

There are mainly three reasons that goats will "paw."

To Get Your Attention: Goats, especially spoiled babies, or adults that were spoiled babies, will paw your leg to get your attention. Most often this behavior is accompanied by nibbling on your clothes or your fingers. This generally means, "Treat, Please!" or "PET ME NOW!"

Hormones: Bucks will paw the ground in frustration when they can't get to a doe through the fence. This is generally accompanied by blabbering of the lips and tongue and lots of vocalizations. You will see a buck paw and kick out their legs as part of their pre-mating activity. Does in heat will sometimes paw the ground as well, and act "bucky." Does in labor will paw the ground as they prepare for kidding. She might also be pawing for the third reason...

To "Fluff" the Bed: It really doesn't matter if the goat is getting ready to lie in the grass, on a shelf, in the dirt, or in fluffy bedding. Goats often paw their sleeping area before they lay down. Mostly likely, this is an instinct that was ingrained in them thousands of years ago. Perhaps they are digging down to get to the cool sand.

Climbing and Playing

Goats are naturally curious, and goats of all ages LOVE to climb. I provide many spools, stumps, barrels and shelves and pallets of many levels in all of my goat yards. We also have tons of Little Tykes slides, cubes, houses and tables for goats to explore. It's important to provide plenty of options for goats so that they do not get bored, and also because a goat will choose to nap on a raised shelf or platform over the ground every time.

Babies are so energetic and they bounce and jump and run all around all the time. If a particularly happy mood strikes the herd, you might see old and young alike bounce down the hill to the pasture, kicking their feet out from side to side and hopping. It's just about the best feeling in the world to know your goats are happy and healthy.

Head Butting

Goats headbutt to display dominance over other goats. The process of gaining position in a herd is incredibly interesting to me, and so...this section will be long, but hopefully you will find it worth the read.

Inside every herd, whether you have two goats or a hundred, there is a hierarchy or official status, for every goat. The status is only truly known by the goats, but it can be observed and noted by humans if you watch long enough. Let's start small as an example, rather than tackling a huge herd. To explain the concept of hierarchies, I will tell you a story.

Let's pretend that I have three goats, Precious, Trixie and Tator, and they are all does in my herd. To start I only have three does, but these does have never lived together before and therefore, do not know each other. As soon as I get them home and into the goat yard, they size each other up by sniffing each other. Soon, they begin head butting each other. As the oldest and most regal doe, Precious decides that she is the Herd Queen. Trixie decides that she wants to be the Herd Queen so she challenges Precious for position. After several hours, and maybe a bloody head or two, Precious has won her status as Herd Queen and so...she is. Trixie falls in line after Precious because Tator is still a baby and is very meek, and Tator has decided not to challenge her position and so she stays at the bottom of the heirarchy of the little herd of three. Times goes on with Precious as Herd Queen, Trixie as second in command, and Tator bringing up the rear, and things are good.

Trixie has been bred and as time grows near to her delivery date, she decides to challenge Precious for Herd Queen status again. She does this to gain a better position for her and for her kids. Try as she might to bump Precious off her pedestal, she fails and again takes the position of second in command and waits for her babies to be born. As she is waiting, a new doe, Kat, arrives to join the herd. Kat is also bred and she is also used to being a queen. She challenges Precious for Herd Queen status. They butt heads all day long, but Kat fails and Precious is the victor as she is much too powerful and regal to have any doe above her in status. Kat, unwilling to concede to Precious, splits off and starts her own clique and takes Tator with her. Now, there is still one herd, but within that herd there are two cliques or family units. One clique consists of Precious and Trixie (and her babies) and the other clique consists of Kat (and her babies) and Tator.

When the babies are born, the heirarchy gets tossled again, because the mommas leave to stay in the barn for a few weeks while their babies grow strong enough to go outside and join the herd. When the mommas leave, there are only two does in the herd, Precious and Tator. They both belong to two different cliques but they decide they can tolerate each other for the time being because Tator has already submitted to Precious and is not willing to challenge. When Kat and Trixie rejoin the herd with their babies in tow, Precious tries to keep her Herd Queen status, but the new moms are invigorated and Kat overthrows Precious as herd queen. Now Kat, Kat's babies, and Tator are the ruling clique. Precious, Trixie and Trixie's babies are still a family unit, but Kat and her group rule the goat yard.

This goes ON and ON and ON. Each time a goat leaves, and each time a goat is added you will have challenges in the hierarchy. Don't fret that they will hurt each other. It's TOTALLY NORMAL! And normally, they do not draw blood. Every once in awhile someone will hit another doe hard enough to knock a scur off and it gets a little raw and/or bloody. There have never been any major injuries in my herd from headbutting, but all of my goats are hornless. If you have horns in your herd, all bets are off, and serious injuries can occur.

When your herd gets big enough, you will see the little family units and cliques within your herd. It's amazing to see babies with their moms, grandmas and great grandmas laying together. Equally awesome is seeing two or three goats with no family in the herd banding together and creating their own clique. Goats are truly amazing and interesting animals and they are SO MUCH FUN to watch!

PS...The above story was fictional, but yes, those are all goats that I once owned. Precious and Trixie are still in my herd and Precious is still the Queen. =)

Other Interesting Goat Behaviors

1. Goat are extremely intelligent, and are also extremely motivated by food. That being said, you can teach goats lots of tricks and commands and get an appropriate response. Researchers at the Queen Mary University of London once taught goats to solve a puzzle intended for primates with amazing results. They repeated the same puzzle to the goats ten months later and they did even better. Needless to say, they also have incredible memories.

2. You can teach goats their names and to respond to simple commands like "get up," "get down," and "come." When I milk, I always milk in the same order every day. This year (2017) I have eight does in my milk string. First Chai comes to the gate to be let out into the milk parlor. When Dido hears the stanchion unlatch she comes to the gate to be let into the milk parlor. I reinforce the order by saying their name to assure them that it's their turn to be milked. Their motivation is food, obviously, as they are allowed to eat as much grain as they want while they are being milked. Then comes Precious, then Diva, then Jessie, then Airianna, then Cleopatra, and finally Delilah. They all know their order, and they all come to line up every morning and every night. Diva prefers to eat from the wrong side of the stand, so she usually goes around the front first and starts munching until I tell her, "Diva! Get up!" and she hops right up on the stanchion to be milked.

3. I was talking with a breeder once and he was talking about how his goats prefer to drink from yellow buckets. Intrigued, I did a scientific research study on my own herd to see which color of bucket they preferred to drink from. I offered six identical 2 gallon buckets of different colors and rotated the position of each bucket twice per day. I weighed the bucket when I set it out, and weighed it again when I changed the water and recorded the data. They do prefer YELLOW!

4. Goats rarely pass gas out the back end, but they do burp often, especially when they are chewing their cud.

5. Goats sneeze when they sense danger to alert the other members of the herd.

6. Although I have no personal experience with potty training goats, I have known some breeders who have done it semi-successfully. I don't think it would be very hard to train a goat to pee in a certain spot, but I doubt I could train them to poop there. Poop seems to fall out at the most inopportune times, where ever the goat is.

7. We have recently been providing goats to a local yoga studio for Goat Yoga, where the goats get to interact with humans and exhibit more of their silly behaviors. I mentioned before that goats love to climb and be up higher than the ground. Yoga provides a perfect opportunity for the goats to jump on the yogi's backs and frolic around the studio. It's a great time with lots of laughing. If a goat jumps on your back, you should be honored, because that's how goats say. . . you are my family.

ASSESSING GOAT HEALTH

I always tell new goat owners that the secret to raising goats is to just pay attention. That is easier said than done, and honestly, it takes practice to notice changes in behavior that will tell you something is wrong. This section will provide a primer to assess your goat's health by observation of their behaviors and symptoms.

General Alertness- Goats ears should be erect and alert. The tail should be up more than down. There should be a gleam in their eyes and a general erectness throughout their whole bodies. If a goat is depressed you will see the opposite symptoms, but don't confuse sleepiness with actual depression.

Bleats- Goats are quiet when they are content. They still make noises regularly, but you can learn to distinguish a distress bleat from a HELLO bleat. Goats who are coming into estrus can be VERY noisy.

Coat and Skin- Coats should be shiny and lustrous. Skin should be supple, and free of blemishes and flakes.

Membrane Color- The eyelids and gums should be bright pink. Pale eyelids indicate anemia, which is usually caused by intestinal parasites. You will learn more about FAMACHA testing later.

Body Condition- Goats should be neither thin, nor fat. Either extreme can indicate problems. Open (unbred) does tend to gain weight as they hit one year of age and can become overconditioned, and tend to lose body mass and become underconditioned as they hit the peak of their lactations after kidding. It's important to gradually increase feed as a doe reaches her due date, kids and starts to lactate. Her body requires more feed when she is working. There is a great educational video on assessing body condition on the ADGA website. Many new goat owners confuse "hay belly" with bloat or a goat being too fat. If the goat has a big belly full of hay but otherwise acts normal, she is fine. The belly is not even considered when you are assessing body condition. Bloat is a condition where the rumen is out of balance and usually in an acidic state causing painful gas and bloating. I've seen it on my farm once. There was cud flying everywhere and the doe was in extreme pain and screaming. It was easily cured and I'll tell you how to cure it later.

Appetite- Goats are browsers and are usually eating or chewing their cud most of the day. If a goat is not chewing her cud regularly this could indicate a problem with the digestive system.

Pain- Goats will grind their back teeth if they are in pain. Do not mistake chewing cud for grinding of the teeth. If they are grinding you can audibly hear it from a few feet away.

Temperature- Normal goat temperature, taken rectally, should be about 103° F. High temperatures indicate a fever most likely caused by an infection. Low temperatures can indicate that the body is shutting down. Goats, including babies, will go off feed if their body temperature is lower than 100°F.

Heart Rate and Respiration- Heart rate should be 70-90 beats per minute. You can check heart rate between the ribs and the elbow. Respirations should be 12-20 breaths per minute.

Rumen Contractions- As the goat ruminates, you should be able to hear contractions which sounds like a stomach growl. Goats should have one or two contractions per minute. If you put your ear to their bellies you can easily hear them.

Waste- Adult droppings should be dark brown, round, firm and fairly dry. Urine should be light-medium yellow to clear.

When you Suspect Something is Wrong

1. Don't panic. Unless the goat is mortally injured or actively dying, you still have time to help her .

2. The first thing to do is to take the goats temperature. If you call your vet or your mentor it's the first thing they are going to ask you, and knowing her temperature will rule out a whole heap of issues. Use a digital thermometer from the dollar store and lubricant to take her core temperature and record.

3. Is she off feed?

4. Is her waste normal?

5. Are her membranes pink?

6. Note any other symptoms you are seeing using the guide above and call your vet or goat mentor.

DISEASES AND DISORDERS

This is not, in any way, an exhaustive list of diseases and disorders of goats, but I am listing the most common ones here. I have left out a discussion of parasites here, as it will be discussed in a later section, but I am including the clinical effects of parasites. We will also not be covering treatments here, as I will cover those later in the Medication section. You should become familiar with the signs and symptoms of the following diseases and disorders in goats.

Abortion- There are many reasons that a doe would abort her kids, and it generally happens 3-6 weeks before her due date. Most often it is caused by chlamydia, toxoplasma gondii, Q-fever, border disease, listeriosis, neospora caninum, camplobacteriosis, akbane disease, and brucellosis. Abortion could also be caused by various nutritional deficiencies, ingestion of toxic plants, and improper feeding, as well as a heavy worm load. It is also possible that a doe aborts due to getting hit very hard by another doe. It is important to find the cause of a spontaneous abortion so that you can treat other pregnant does if the cause is infectious. Take the fetal tissue for a necropsy as soon as possible to your vet or university lab.

Acetonemia (Ketosis)- The metabolic imbalance caused by feeding an improper balance of feed. If left untreated, it will often progress to enterotoxemia (see below) which can cause death. Symptoms include depression, going off feed, general malaise, staggering, heavy breathing and grinding of the teeth. The easiest symptom a goat can express if she is in ketosis is that her urine will smell sweet and fruity due to excess ketones.

Anemia- The most common cause of anemia is an infestation of intestinal parasites, most commonly, the barberpole worm. Anemia is evident when the mucous membranes of the eyes and the gums are pale.

Brucellosis- Bacterial infection. Symptoms include abortion in late pregnancy, inflamed uterus, and retained placenta in does. In bucks, symptoms include infertility, swollen testicles, and swollen joints.

Bloat- There are two kinds of bloat. Bloat occurs when a excess of gas gets trapped in the rumen. Frothy bloat is more common, and occurs when the goat eats damp hay or overeats lush pasture, particularly in the springtime. Both conditions are life threatening and must be treated ASAP. Symptoms include a distended, hard belly accompanied by the animal stomping her feet, bleating loudly, and walking stiff legged.

Caprine Arthritis Encephalitis (CAE)- CAE is a virus that is reported to be present in up to 80% of herds in America. It is highly contagious and transferable to other goats via bodily fluids. Some goats are asymptomatic for their entire lives, so you would never know they had it unless you test for it. When CAE flares it is most commonly identified by weight loss, poor hair condition, and swollen joints particularly in the carpal, hocks, and stifle. There is no cure or vaccine for this disease.

Caseous Lymphadenitis (CL)- Caseous lymphadenitis is caused by the bacterium coryne and bacterium pseudotuberculosis. The disease causes boils or cheesy lumps in the lymph nodes, most commonly occurring on the neck and under the jaw, but they can pop up near any lymph node. CL is mostly a benign disease, but it is highly contagious to other goats and a major nuisance.

Collibacillosis/collisopticemia (E. coli)- E.coli is a bacteria that thrives in unclean areas, and most often affects newborn kids. Symptoms include a watery bright yellow or white scours (diarrhea), hunched appearance, and fever or subnormal (low) temperature.

Conjunctivitis (Pink Eye)- Pinkeye can be caused by infectious or non-infectious organisms. First symptoms include red, runny, irritated eyes which you may not notice. As the conjunctivitis progresses, the iris of the affected eye(s) get cloudy. Failure to treat the eye(s) at this stage could result in blindness and rupture of the eye. If the eye ruptures, the infection could spread to the brain and kill the goat.

Dermatitis- There are many things that cause dermatitis, because dermatitis itself is a broad definition for "skin irritation." Dermatitis can be caused by contact with certain plants and substances, insect bites, mange mites, and vitamin and mineral deficiencies.

Enterotoxaemia- Enterotoxaemia is also commonly known as the overeating disease, but it is actually caused by toxic levels of clostridium perfringens type D (CD), which is normally found inside the normal flora of the rumen. Under certain conditions (too much grain, too much milk, too little roughage, heavy parasite load) the CD rapidly reproduces inside the rumen and causes acidosis. Without speedy treatment, death can occur suddenly. Onset of symptoms generally include watery and/or bloody diarrhea, abdominal discomfort, loss of appetite and subnormal temperature.

Foot Rot- Foot rot or Hoof rot is caused when the goat's hooves are exposed to extreme wet conditions without the opportunity for the feet to dry out. The moisture causes the subcutaneous tissues to soften and the hoof walls to thin and crack, which lets in bacteria and causes an infection. Ulcers, abscesses, inflammation, and fractures will eventually lead to lameness and loss of body weight.

Heat stress- Goats are extremely hardy animals, but they do not sweat. When goats are exposed to extremely high temperatures, they can suffer from heat stress and die of heat stroke. Symptoms include extreme panting, salivating and/or foaming, and high body temperature.

Hypocalcemia- Commonly known as milk fever. Usually shows itself during labor indicated by weak contractions and incomplete pushing. If not treated in labor, the condition can intensify shortly after a doe kids and the doe will no longer be able to stand. Treatment must begin quickly, or the doe can fall into a coma and die. This condition is caused by a lack of sufficient calcium in the body due to improper nutrition during gestation. Calcium is robbed from the bones of the doe which is further intensified by the demands of growing kids and brings her body over the edge as the doe starts to produce milk.

Johnne's Disease- Also known as Paratuberculosis, a contagious, chronic and sometimes fatal infection that primarily affects the small intestine of ruminants. It is spread through fecal to oral contact and is most commonly seen in goats over two years of age, although a goat can have the disease and be asymptomatic for its entire life. Symptoms include extreme weight loss and wasting that may or may not be accompanied by diarrhea, and degradation of the quality of the coat.

Laminitis/Founder- Goat becomes lame and reluctant to move; there is a fever, and all four feet are hot to the touch. Laminitis is caused by overeating or sudden access to concentrates, high-grain and low-roughage diets, or high-protein diets. Laminitis can also develop as a complication of acute infections.

Listeriosis- A brain-stem nerve disorder caused by improper feeding, in particular, feeding too much grain and too little roughage. Symptoms include depression, decreased appetite, fever, leaning or stumbling or moving in one direction only, head pulled to flank with rigid neck, facial paralysis on one side, blindness, slack jaw, and drooling. Listeriosis can be mistaken for rabies.

Mastitis- Condition of the udder caused by contamination of staphylococci, streptococci, E. coli, Mycoplasma agalactiae, M. arginini, Yeast or Fungi. Symptoms include watery/chunky milk, blood tinged milk, hard hot udder, reduced milk production. Mastitis can be acute or chronic.

Mange- Most mange is caused by sarcoptic mites. Mites are invisible to the naked eye and a skin scraping to verify is necessary. Skin becomes flaky with itchiness. Hair loss occurs with the thickening and hardening of the skin.

Mycoplasma- Mycoplasmas are slow-growing one celled organisms that are categorized somewhere between a bacterium and a virus. Mycoplasmas can cause serious illness and death in goats. There are various strains that cause a variety of problems including respiratory pleuropneumonia, arthritis, mastitis, conjunctivitis, and septicemia. Supportive therapies are available, but most recommend culling of animals with mycoplasma infections because there is currently no cure and the infection is highly contagious.

Parasitic Gastroenteritis- A heavy parasitic load left untreated will often result in parasitic gastroenteritis, which makes way for enterotoxaemia and death. Symptoms that the goat is losing the battle with parasites includes severe anemia, then diarrhea, followed by emaciation and sometimes bottle jaw, which is a watery swelling of the jawline.

Polio- See Trace Element Deficiency

Rabies- The disease develops usually after 20-60 days of bite, but not less than 10 days of bite. The goat becomes strange in behavior and there is frothing and salivation. The goat does not eat or drink, slowly becomes paralyzed and dies within 10 days of onset of disease.

Ringworm- Fungal infection. Symptoms include inflammation of hair follicles, falling of hairs, circular lesions on the face, shoulder, neck, and eyes, irritation and rubbing, thick crusts or scales may appear.

Tetanus- Tetanus can occur after the bacteria, clostridium tetani, enters a wound caused by disbudding, castrating, tattooing, hoof trimming, or an accidental wound the goat received. Symptoms include stiffness of the body and reluctance to move, difficulty opening the mouth and seizures.

Trace Element Deficiency- Deficiency of a trace element can cause serious problems and even death, but most of the deficiencies can be easily cured. The trick becomes identifying which elements are needed according to the symptoms. We will talk more about trace element and mineral requirements in the Feeding Section. Below are the most common deficiencies.

Copper Deficiency- Symptoms include course coat, dandruff, coppery red deposits on coat (especially on black), Loss of coat luster, weight loss, general unthriftiness.

Selenium Deficiency (White Muscle Disease)- Symptoms are most evident in newborn kids and include weak kids, weak legs and feet, and delayed standing and walking. Selenium is always administered with Vitamin E (BoSe). Adult symptoms of selenium deficiency include blind staggering, weakness in the legs, inability to conceive, abortions, retained placenta.

Thiamine (B1) Deficiency (Goat Polio)- Symptoms are similar to listeriosis and include excitability, stargazing, uncoordinated staggering and/or weaving, circling, diarrhea, muscle tremors, and blindness. Always treat for both.

Vitamin E Deficiency- Same symptoms as selenium deficiency. Always treat for both.

Zinc Deficiency- Most common symptom of zinc deficiency is a very flaky skin and hair loss in patches over the body that is not caused by mites. I have several does in my herd who have a hard time storing enough zinc when they are pregnant. I must keep on top of their zinc needs or they will lose their coats!

Upper Respiratory Infections and Pneumonia- Upper respiratory infections, also known as sinusitis, generally occurs after a large temperature swing in the weather. Symptoms include clear to white nasal discharge from one or both nostrils, coughing, sneezing and mild respiratory distress. Goats can generally fight off an upper respiratory infection without antibiotics, but you must watch the goat closely to make sure the infection does not move into the lungs, causing pneumonia. In pneumonia nasal discharge is yellow or green with sneezing, coughing, mild to severe respiratory distress and fever. Pneumonia is also contagious, and goats must be quarantined until all symptoms disappear.

Urinary Calculi (UC)- Urinary Calculi is sometimes called Urinary Stones. Generally, only male goats get stones. Does may get stones, but their urethra is short and wide, and they can pass the stones without issue. In bucks and wethers, their urethras are long and winding. Calcium deposits build up in the body and stones develop and block the urethra. Symptoms that your buck has UC include tail twitching, restlessness, anxiety, and a "hunched-up" body posture as the goat strains to urinate. Treatments exist, including surgery, but they are very rarely successful. Usually the bladder bursts and the buck most often die an extremely painful death.

Many believe that feeding alfalfa to bucks causes UC. That is not entirely true. Bucks and wethers require a BALANCED diet just like does do, and feeding alfalfa is not the entire issue. (More on proper feeding later.)

UC has recently become a huge problem because of the castrating practices of some breeders. In an effort to move animals out, breeders are castrating WAY too early. I've heard of some that castrate at 2-6 weeks of age so they can move them to their new homes quickly to lessen their workload. These wethers have an extremely high chance of dying from UC, and I have taken dozens of calls over the years asking me for help with little wethers who have developed UC. Sadly, there is usually no hope.

When you remove the testicles, testosterone production stops, which is what helps the urethra grow. The bigger the urethra at castration, the easier it is for the goat to pass stones, should they develop, through normal urination. I do not castrate before 12 weeks of age for this very reason, and I have NEVER had a single issue with UC, neither on my farm or at a wether's new home.

White Muscle Disease- See Trace Element Deficiency

MEDICATIONS

This is not an exhaustive list of medications that can be used on goats. I'm including only the most effective and the ones that I use or would use in my herd. Some of the medications below are not made for goats at all but through the diligent research and experiments of myself and fellow breeders, we can determine the effectiveness and useful dosages of the following medications. Parasites and dewormers will be discussed in a later section.

. . .

IM- (Intermuscular Injection)
Injection given in the muscle of the animal. Hormones are given IM.
Sub-Q- (Subcutaneous Injection)
Injection given right under the skin of the animal. All injections can be given Sub-Q, except hormones, which go IM.

1 CC (Cubic Centimeter) is the same as 1 ML (Milliliter)
1 teaspoon = 5 cc
1 tablespoon = 15 cc

Adrenaline

Epinephrine (Adrenaline)- RX Only. A must have for every farm. If given immediately, counters anaphylactic shock due to injection reaction. If goat collapses within minutes of giving any injection, use epinephrine to save them at a rate of 1cc per 100 lbs.

Antibiotics

Oxytetracycline- Broad spectrum antibiotic. Used to cure pink eye, uterine infections, navel ill in kids and bacterial mastitis. The non-stinging version can be found under the brand name Bio-Mycin 200 , while the original version is called LA-200. Correct dosage is 1cc per 30 lbs daily for three days. Do not use with Penicillin. Milk withholding time= 18 days.

Procaine Penicillin G (Pen G)- Good for bacterial infections like pneumonia. Administer 1 cc per 15 lbs twice a day for at least 5 days or until all symptoms disappear. Do not use in conjunction with Oxytet. Milk withholding time=20 days.

Trimethoprim/Sulfaethoxazole (TMP/SMZ)- RX Only. I use these pills to combat coccidia. Can also be used for infections. Dose 1 pill orally to adults daily. Kids get 1/2 pill. I like to crush them first and adhere the powder to animal crackers. Milk withholding time=8 days .

Sulfadimenthoxine- Technically an antibacterial. The brand I use is called DiMethox 12.5%. Great for battling coccidia, especially in kids. Dose orally at 1cc per 5 lbs daily for 5 days.

Painkillers

Aspirin 325mg- Fever reducer, pain killer, anti-inflammatory. Give 1 aspirin orally per 10 lbs. Milk withholding time=24 hours

Ibuprofen- Fever reducer, pain killer, anti-inflammatory. Give double the human dose. Milk withholding time=24 hours

Banamine (Fluxixin Meglumine)- RX Only- Fever reducer, pain killer, anti-inflammatory. 1cc per 100 lbs. Do not use for more than 3 days in a row. Milk withholding time=4 days

Vitamins and Minerals

Selenium Tocopherol (Bo-Se)- Rx Only. Used to combat white muscle disease, selenium deficiency, and improve fertility. Dose at 1cc per 40 lbs before breeding season and 2 weeks before kidding. Weak newborns dose 1/4cc. Milk withholding time=24 hours.

Vitamin B Complex Injectable- B Complex contains thiamine, riboflavin, niacin/niacinamide, vitamin B6, vitamin B12, folic acid, and pantothenic acid. A must have for any goat farmer. Used to stimulate appetite, soothe rumens, combat shipping fever, and to perk up any sick animal. B Complex is water soluable and is metabolized by goats very quickly. Dose at a rate of 1cc per 20 lbs.

Red Cell (Iron Supplement)- Oral supplement used to stimulate the creation of red blood cells in anemic animals. Give in conjunction with dewormers at a rate of 1cc per 20 lbs.

Zinpro TruCare 4 (Zinc, Manganese, Copper, Cobalt)- Top dress mineral for feed. Used to combat dermatitis due to zinc deficiency. Use directions on bag. Personally, I daily dose each affected goat individually by mixing the mineral with molasses to make a paste and sandwich the mixtures between animal cookies or Ritz crackers.

Hormones

Prostaglanin (Lutalyse)- RX Only Used to bring does into estrus, abort an unwanted pregnancy, or to induce labor. To bring does into estrus, dose 1 cc IM. Doe will come into standing heat 65-75 hours later. To abort an unwanted pregnancy, wait TEN DAYS from the date the doe was exposed to the buck and dose 2cc IM. To induce labor, dose 1/2cc to 2 cc with delivery in 24-60 hours.

Oxytocin- RX Only. Used to cause uterine contractions. You must be absolutely certain that the doe is completely dialated before using this hormone or you are at risk of causing irreparable damage to the doe. Use to strengthen contractions, expel the afterbirth or to clamp down the uterus to stop bleeding.

Dexamethozone- RX Only. Used to induce labor, and also to stimulate lung and system development in newborns. Dex is an anadrenal corticosteroid, and anti-inflammatory and a pain reliever. Dosage is 1cc per 20 lbs IM injection.

Vaccinations

Please note: We no longer vaccinate our herd due to various reasons. Instead, we use the antitoxins as needed.

Clostridium Perfringes C&D Bactern -Toxoid (CD&T)- The CD&T vaccination protects goats against enterotoxaemia and tetanus. The accurate dose is 2cc per kid or adult animal. Kids should be vaccinated at 6 weeks of age, and again at 10 weeks of age. Adults should be vaccinated once per year. *Caution-Certain brands and batches of this vaccine has been shown to be largely ineffective at protecting against enterotoxaemia. This vaccine usually causes knots at the injection site which may burst. There has also recently (2017) been reports of bad batches of CD&T causing death and near death injuries in kids.*

Clostridium Perfringes C&D Bactern - C&D Antitoxin- This antitoxin should be used if enterotoxaemia is suspected. Young kids should be given 3cc of antitoxin up to 3 times per day to stop enterotoxaemia. Adults should be given 10-15 cc of antitoxin to stop enterotoxaemia.

Tetanus - Antitoxin- Provides protection for up to ten days against tetanus after castration, tattoo, disbudding or accidental injury. 1/2 cc for kids and 1 cc for adults.

CONTROLLING PARASITES

Controlling parasites first begins with understanding them.

- A parasite is an organism that feeds, grows and reproduces by taking nutrients (mainly, blood) from its host, in this case, a goat.
- Parasites propagate in wet, undrained pastures and dirty pens.
- Parasites generally only attack one particular area or part of an animal. This is precisely what makes them so deadly.
- Most parasites are incredibly contagious, because eggs are constantly being shed off through the animal's waste. This is how the parasite assures its survival. Other goats pick up the cast off eggs in the pasture.
- It is estimated that it takes three years to eradicate worms from a pasture by letting it rest. Rotational grazing is suggested.

Stomach Worms: The Mighty Barberpole

The biggest threat to a goat's health and life is the barberpole worm (Haemonchus contortus) or HC. The barberpole worm is a blood sucking parasite that attaches itself to the inside lining of the abomasum, which is the true stomach of the goat. Adult worms are 3/4" to 1" long. Female barberpoles are red and white striped (like a barberpole) and the male barberpole is red. You will most likely never see a barberpole worm, either alive or dead, because they are not usually shed and rarely visible in the goat's waste. The only evidence you may see would be eggs when doing a fecal exam, but eggs are not always shed off, making it even more difficult to diagnose. There are also conflicting opinions among veterinarians about what constitutes an infestation, and what is an "acceptable load."

Barberpole worms reproduce inside the abomasum, and the population is always growing. They feed off the goats red blood cells inside the abomasum, causing the goat to become anemic, which can quickly cause death. Symptoms of a barberpole infestation includes anemia, followed by scours (diarrhea) and weight loss, and finally emaciation and death due to parasitic gastroenteritis. Due to the difficulty in diagnosing, the trick becomes catching the goat becoming anemic before the other symptoms follow. The test to check for anemia is called FAMACHA, and you will learn how to do that in the next section.

Treatment for barberpole worm:
Cydectin Pour On Cattle Dewormer dosed at 1 cc per 20 lbs ORALLY, Once every 10 days for 30 days. This schedule is most likely to catch all life cycles of the barberpole worm, including killing off all the eggs.
Milk Withholding: None.

Please note: Dosing pregnant does with Cydectin has been observed to cause birth defects in some cases, especially in early pregnancy, so use with caution. Ivomec and copper are a much better choice for deworming bred does.

Lungworms

Lungworms burrow into the bronchioles of the lungs causing inflammation, phlegm and coughing. Persistent cough is usually the first sign. Lungworms are extremely hard to diagnose. The only way to find lungworms in the feces is if the goat coughs some up and then swallows them.

Treatment for Lungworms:
Ivomec 1% given orally at 1cc per 33 lbs. Official milk withdrawal is 36 days. Personally, I withhold for only 7 days.

Liver Flukes

The liver is responsible for filtering toxins and waste products from the blood. Liver flukes burrow tunnels into the liver. The liver quickly tries to repair itself causing massive scar tissue, which is not operational. As the scar tissue grows, the toxins and waste that a healthy liver filters out build up in the body causing damage to other organs and the brain.

Symptoms of liver flukes include rough coat, weight loss, poor milk production, "bottle jaw", anemia, chronic diarrhea and stupor.

Treatment for liver flukes:
Fenbendazole (SafeGuard, Panacur) given orally at 4X the dose for horses/cattle.
Milk withholding 4 days.

Coccidia

Coccidia is a one-celled intestinal parasite caused by overcrowding, dirty wet pens, and unclean water. The organism is spread by fecal to oral contact and can spread rapidly to other goats. All goats have some small levels of cocci inside their bodies which are constantly being fought off by a healthy immune system. Cocci infestation is most common in kids, but all goats can be overwhelmed by it.

First symptoms are usually, but not always, diarrhea and sometimes, fever. Dehydration occurs rapidly. If left unchecked, the goat can easily die, or cocci can cause permanent damage to the intestinal lining and prohibit the goat from absorbing nutrients for the rest of its life.

Treatment for Coccidia:
For Kids: Di-Methoox Concentrated Solution 12.5% dosed orally at 1cc per 5 lbs daily for 5 days
or
TMP/SMZ dosed orally at 1 pill for adult goats once daily for 7 days. Milk Withholding 8 days.

Tapeworms

Tapeworms are one of only two parasites that you can see in the feces, so they are easily diagnosed. Adult worms are white, ribbon-like and/or segments like grains of rice. Tapeworm eggs are small and triangular in shape. Tapeworms give little threat to adult animals, but they can obtruct the digestive systems of young kids and cause issues, and even death.

Treatment for tapeworms:
Fenbendazole (SafeGuard, Panacur) given orally at 4X the dose for horses/cattle.
Milk withholding 4 days.

Pinworms
Pinworms are small, threadlike parasites that look like white, wiggly, curly hairs around the anus of the goat. They cause no actual threat to a goat's health but can be annoying when you are milking a doe and see pinworms a few inches from your face. True story.

Treatment for pinworms:
Fenbendazole (SafeGuard, Panacur) given orally at 4X the dose for horses/cattle.
Milk withholding 4 days.

Lice
Lice are the only bugs that infest goats that you can see with the naked eye. Part the coat down to the skin, particularly along the backbone. Lice and nits, alike, may be found. Rough coat and patchy, flaky skin and hair loss are symptoms.

Treatment for Lice:
Bathe and groom goat as necessary. Shave if weather permits.
Ivomec 1% given orally at 1cc per 33 lbs. Official milk withdrawal is 36 days. Personally, I withhold for only 7 days. There is also an over the counter product called SyLence. Follow directions on box.

Mites
Mites are not visible with the naked eye, and must be confirmed under a microscope. Symptoms of mites includes patchy, flaky skin, thickened skin in places, and hair loss. Do not confuse a case of mites for zinc deficiency which looks VERY similar. Confirm mites with a skin scraping or treat for both.

Treatment for Mites:
Ivomec 1% given orally at 1cc per 33 lbs. Official milk withdrawal is 36 days. Personally, I withhold for only 7 days.

Identifying Parasites

A couple of years ago, I broke down and bought a microscope to run fecal exams on my goats. I can't say that I've used it extensively, but it sure has come in handy in many situations. It's not difficult to learn to do a simple float so that you can at least identify what you are dealing with. I bought the Know Thine Enemy Fecal Test Kit from Maggidans Minis. The kit is easy to understand with tons of informative information and pictures included. As of yet, I have not used the McMaster Slide which was included, but I have not yet been interested in the actual loads of worms, only the identification of the worm that is causing the problem. On the surface, the kit looks to be expensive, but it will pay for itself quickly. I highly recommend this kit to anyone who wants to do their own fecal exams to get results sooner and save the costs on exams from the vet.

Here are a couple blog posts from my farm site that you may find helpful, when identifying parasites with a microscope:

How to Run a Fecal Examination (Blog from 01/13/2014 Twin Willows Farm)
http://www.twinwillowsfarm.net/1/post/2014/01/how-to-run-a-fecal-exam.html

How to Make Fecal Floatation Solution (Blog from 1/14/2014 Twin Willows Farm)
http://www.twinwillowsfarm.net/1/post/2014/01/how-to-make-fecal-floatation-solution.html

Now, let's learn about the most important test in your goat keeping arsenal, FAMACHA.

FAMACHA

What is FAMACHA? It stands for FAffa MAlan CHArt, and is a method of testing for determining parasite loads in goats and sheep so that we can know when to treat them. You learned in the last section about the deadliest parasite, The Barberpole. This is the only reasonable way that we can combat this horrible parasite, and if done regularly, you will be able to save many lives.

FAMACHA testing takes two things: practice and persistence, and both go hand in hand. If we practice being persistent about testing our goats regularly, we can prevent the barberpole from taking over. As stated in the previous section, the barberpole worm causes anemia in goats, which is usually the first sign of infestation and what sets the goat spiraling towards its eventual death. I don't mean to scare, but then I do...because it's just that serious.

Some people like to make it seem that FAMACHA testing is difficult and that you need to be formally trained in order to use it. Honestly, FAMACHA is a very simple method of observing and recording the color of the individual goat's mucous membranes. The inside lower lid of the eye is the easiest and most available to check, and that is where the testing is done.   The other areas to watch include the gums and inside the mouth, and the perineal area (around the anus in bucks, around the anus and vulva in does). The eyes give the best, most accurate reading.

The **FAMACHA Scorecard*** CAN BE used as a guide to check the goats score, but a STRONG WORD OF CAUTION. It is less important to know the actual score on the card than it is to know what your goat's membranes look like when they have no worm load (i.e. are healthy). A perfectly healthy parasite-free member of your herd might never obtain a FAMACHA score of 1 (Optimal) if that color is not normal for her. That being said, it's most important to check your goats membranes regularly, and catch any changes in the color before it becomes a problem. Check often!

On my farm, most of my animals stay in the 2 (Acceptable) score when they are healthy. Because I know my goats' healthy scores, as a rule I only deworm them when they hit about 3.5 (between Borderline and Dangerous). If they are in this range I generally dose once and then recheck in ten days. Depending on their scores after the first dose, I may dose again. If they are a 4 or 5 range I use the full dose schedule for 30 days and recheck. For medication and dosing information, visit the Controlling Parasites page.

IMPORTANT: I no longer recommend a maintenance dose of dewormer. Please do not use a dewormer if it's not necessary! Many worms become resistant to the dewormers we have used because their life cycles are short and they EVOLVE very quickly and adjust and adapt to things that are meant to harm them. This makes it very hard for the animal medicine producers to keep up with the ever-changing landscape of what works and what doesn't. For now, (or until the worms "get smart" again) I've given you the best information I have on which dewormers to use and their effective dosages.

*Obviously, it would do me no good to show you a FAMACHA color scorecard in a black and white book, but you can download and print a color FAMACHA Scorecard on my website at http://www.thegoatchick.com/famacha-testing.html

TOXIC AND POISONOUS PLANTS

This list is controversial, because some breeders swear that some of the plants on this list are not poisonous at all. Please remember that too much of ANYTHING is not a GOOD thing, so take this list with a grain of salt, and be observant of the plants and weeds that occur around your goat yard and the plants they have access to.

African Rue
Andromeda (related to foxglove)
Avocado- South American
Avocado leaves
Avocado- Fuarte
Azalea
Brouwer's Beauty Andromeda
Boxwood
Burning Bush berries
Calotropis
Cassava (manioc)
China Berry Trees
Choke Cherries
Choke Cherry Leaves
Datura
Dog Hobble
Dumb Cane (diffenbachia)
Euonymus Bush berries
False Tansy
Fiddleneck
Flixweed
Fusha
Holly Trees/Bushes
Ilysanthes floribunda
Japanese pieris (extremely toxic)
Japanese Yew

Lantana
Larkspur
Lasiandra
Lilacs
Lily of the Valley (Pieris Japonica)
Lupine
Madreselva (Spain) patologia renal
Maya-Maya
Monkhood
Milkweed
Mountain Laurel
Nightshade
Oleander
Pieris Japonica (extremely toxic)
Red Maples
Rhododendron
Rhubarb leaves
Tu Tu (Coriaria arborea)
Wild Cherry
Yew

FEEDING

Ahh feeding. Seems so simple, right? Throw some hay and water at a goat and they live, right? Well, probably. Honestly, I am just now, after seven years, starting to understand this subject and I know I still have so much to learn, but in the interest of being transparent and trying to help you to understand how FEED FUELS THE SYSTEM, I will tell you what I know.

We have already been over how the digestive system works. If you missed it, you can catch it again in the section on Goat Anatomy. I also previously overviewed feeding in Prepare for Goats, but now we want to get down to the nitty gritty. Anyone can have a few backyard goats and throw some feed at them and they will probably sustain themselves on that feed with minimal issues for the rest of their lives. I raise dairy goats, and the purpose of the dairy goat is to...MAKE MILK! Not just any milk...the best milk. And the best milk comes from healthy, sleeked out, balanced, strong dairy animals. To achieve this, we must feed a well-balanced diet to maximize the productive life of the doe.

Diet

Hay and forage make up the main diet of goats and should be available to them at all times. A legume hay, such as alfalfa, is best for lactating does. Alfalfa or alfalfa grass hay should provide 16% protein to the does diet. A high-quality grain with 14-16% protein should also be fed to the doe at a rate of approximately 1 lb for every 3lbs of milk produced. Grass hay can also be used as a doe's main diet if a higher protein (16-18%) grain is used to supplement the lower protein content of the grass hay. Grain intake should be adjusted according to the body condition of the doe and her stage of lactation.
Be careful not to overfeed grain, as feeding too much creates a hazardous and potentially deadly environment in the rumen. All changes in feed intake should be done gradually.

Hay Testing

If you are serious about what your goats are eating, you need to both visually inspect the bales you will be buying, as well as have the hay supply tested. Many times, the hay producer will agree to test the hay at their expense. Many feed stores will send out hay for testing and some even do it free of charge!

Please note: I use the term "good" in the following paragraph to mean, neither fair nor premium quality hay.

When hay is tested, (ask your local ag extension office for lab recommendations) the analysis is going to provide you with three major results that you need to pay attention to. The first result is CRUDE PROTEIN (CP). In a good bale of hay, you want to see AT LEAST 16% CP for lactating does. The second result you should pay attention to is ADF or Acid Detergent Fiber. ADF is the part of the hay that is not digestible by goats, is mostly wasted on the floor of your barn, and is otherwise the inactive portion of a bale. A good bale of hay should contain less than 30 ADF. The last number you want to pay attention to is TDN or Total Digestible Nutrients. This is the actual percentage of the hay that your does will be eating and directly using as their fuel to make all that delicious milk. A good bale of hay should have around 59% TDN.

There are many other numbers you will get when you get your hay analyzed, but I'm not going to discuss them here. For a very thorough explanation of how hay is tested and what the results mean visit http://alfalfa.ucdavis.edu/IrrigatedAlfalfa/pdfs/UCAlfalfa8302ForageQuality_free.pdf.

Elements and Trace Mineral Requirements
Calcium (Ca) and Phosphorus (P)
Calcium and Phosphorus is stored in the skeleton of the doe, and the body has the ability to draw from its stores during times of need. A doe builds up its stores to excess values during pregnancy, and depletes the excess after kidding, so it is important that ample nutrients be provided during this critical time of need. A doe's body requires 7.1 g Ca and 4.9 g P for daily maintenance plus 1.3 g Ca and 1 g P for every kg of milk produced. Ample amounts of Vitamin D help the body retain calcium in the bones.

Magnesium (Mg)

Goats require a daily supply of 1.2 g of Magnesium. Like Ca and P, a goat's magnesium supply can be drawn from the body in times of need. 70% of Magnesium is stored in the bones and teeth, while the other 30% can be found in the blood supply.

Zinc (Zn)

Zinc is found in the hair, skin and enzymes. Exact zinc needs are not well documented, but 10-60 ppm in the feed seems to be satisfactory. Ample zinc helps the body retain copper and iron.

Manganese (Mn)

Manganese is stored in the liver and is essential to a goat's reproductive health. The daily requirement of manganese is 60-90 ppm in the feed.

Iodine (I)

Iodine is stored in the thyroid gland and is essential to a healthy goat's metabolism. Only 0.15mg per day is required but this amount is essential.

Copper (Cu)

Copper aids digestion and utilizes iron in the body. Excess iron in the water supply can often create an imbalance if proper copper is not supplemented. Copper can be provided by bolusing deficient goats.

Sidenote: I recently installed a filter on my barn water source to remove excess iron in our well water. My hope is that the removal of the iron from their water source will help the animals to use other nutrients more efficiently (copper, zinc, selenium), make them healthier, and save money on supplements I give to overcome the excess iron. I will update with results when I have a conclusion. I installed the Camco EVO Premium RV Water Filter.

Selenium (Se)

Selenium is essential to cell metabolism and works in conjunction with Vitamin E. Many areas of the country are deficient in Selenium (Map of Selenium Averages in United States). Even if your area is not technically deficient according to the map, selenium is mostly stored in the soil so the amount of selenium that is contained in plants which grow there is less than what is officially measured in the soil. Selenium can be supplemented by injection, and should be provided several weeks before a doe is due to kid, to make sure the babies are not born deficient.

Iron (Fe)

Iron is stored in the blood and essential to red blood cell production. Daily intake of 75mg is required for lactating does. Iron should be supplemented (Red Cell Iron Supplement) when a goat becomes anemic during heavy parasite load to aid in the repopulation of red blood cells in the blood.

Cobalt (Co)

Cobalt is important to the production of the Vitamin B12. The daily requirement of cobalt is .5 mg.

Sodium (Na)

Goats require a daily supply of 1.5g per day of Sodium, which is equivalent to 3.5 g of salt (sodium chloride).

Potassium (K)

Relatively high values of Potassium are required by goats. Luckily, most forage contains ample amounts in the roughage, but feeding a grain with potassium added will do no harm.

Vitamins

Vitamin A- aids disease resistance and is required for good vision, lactation and reproduction.

Vitamin D- required for the storage of Calcium and Phosphorous in the skeleton.

Vitamin E- works in conjunction with Selenium and Vitamin A.

Vitamin B1 (Thiamin)- helps disease resistance and is essential to the health of the nervous system

Pantothenic acid- important to the formation of enzymes and antibodies

Vitamin B12 (Cyanocobalamin)- directly associated with cobalt and important to the health of the gut

Loose Minerals

Goats generally know what they are lacking when it comes to trace minerals. For this reason, they should have free access to a a good, clean loose mineral at all times. They will eat it when they need it. Keep it clean, dry and accessible in their pen near a clean water source. Below is an example of a good loose mineral blend (Sweetlix Magnum-Milk) for milking does:

Calcium, 7.50%-9.00%
Phosphorus, Min 8.00%
Salt, 10.00%-12.00%
Magnesium, Min 4.50%
Cobalt, Min 240 ppm
Copper, Min 1,750 ppm
Iodine, Min 450 ppm
Manganese, Min 1.25%
Selenium, Min 50 ppm
Zinc, Min 1.25%
Vitamin A, Min 300,000 IU/lb
Vitamin D-3, Min 30,000 IU/lb
Vitamin E, Min 400 IU/lb

HOOF CARE

If you have never trimmed a goat's hooves, it may seem scary, but really it is a very simple and necessary procedure. Keeping your goat's hooves neat and trimmed help keep the feet free from disorder and disease and help keep your goat happy and comfortable. At my farm, we trim our goat's hooves every 4-6 weeks. We find that some goats need their hooves trimmed more often, depending on the individual goat. They generally grow faster if the doe is lactating or pregnant. The key is to check their hooves often and make adjustments as necessary.

The hoof walls, which is the area around the outside of the hoof, grow faster than the goat can wear them down, and so they must be trimmed.

Tools Needed:
Hoof Pick
Hoof Rot Sheers
Fine Rasp

1. Put your goat in the stanchion and feed them some grain to keep them calm and occupied.
2. The first task is to clean the dirt and debris from the hoof with a hoof pick.
3. Next, using hoof rot shears (which is a horrible name for them, but that is actually what they are called) trim the hoof walls so that they are flush to the pads of the toes. You may also need to trim the tips of the toes if they are "elfy." Remember that less is more here, and take your time to make sure you do not take too much too quickly. With really tough hooves, you might need to "chip away" at the walls in small bites to get through them. We find that the older the goat is, the tougher their hooves will be.

4. Once the walls are flush with the soft part of the toes, take a look at the soft heel at the back of the hoof. This may also need trimmed in order to make the hoof level again. I generally leave the heel alone unless it is starting to fold over, like it is in the picture above. This part is always a little scary to me, but think of it as a cuticle or callus. As long as the flesh is still white when you trim, you are safe. If you start seeing pink flesh when you trim, STOP! Pink means you are getting close to blood. If you do draw blood, do not panic, and use some blood stop powder on the wound.

5. The final task in hoof trimming is to check the dewclaws. These may also need trimming, and are similar to trimming the heel. White is ok, and pink means STOP! During show season, we like to use a Dremel on the hooves and dewclaws. This is not necessary, but you may also use a fine rasp to put the final touches on the hoof, and fine tune the levelness of the hoof.

For full color pictures on hoof trimming, visit the Hoof Care section on **www.thegoatchick.com**

GROOMING AND SHOWING

Fitting a Dairy Goat for Show

No matter whether you decide to show your goat or not, it's always a good idea that you know how to groom them. Grooming a goat is called fitting it. It's a very simple process, but it does take some time to do it correctly. The following process should be used to fit a dairy goat for a show. Other breeds of goats may have different requirements.

1. A week before the show, thoroughly brush out and then wash your goat. Removing dirt and residue from the goat before clipping makes the blades work more efficiently. Be sure to dry the coat thoroughly before proceeding.

2. Secure your goat on a stanchion and provide food for the goat to keep her occupied during clipping. Starting at the tail, hold the long hairs of the end of the tail together with your non-dominant hand, and using a 10 blade clipper, clip the free hair of the tail against the grain and towards the head. Be careful not to clip the hairs you are holding in your hand but clear away all the hair around it, along the rump, and up each side of the vulva. Once the tail has been shaved, release the hairs you are holding and square the tip with the clippers to create a fringe. Proceed to shave the goats entire body with the #10 blade going against the grain of the hair. For white goats, some people prefer the #7 blade over the entire body. Fold each leg and lift up to shave the body underneath the shoulder joints, along the brisket and in the crease of the thighs near the udder.

3. As you proceed towards the head to the shoulders and especially the neck and head, be sure to remove the feed pan to keep the hair out of it. I save the head for last because it is usually the most difficult. The trick to getting it done is to work with the goat, and not against her. If she turns her head away from the clippers, shave the portion of the head that is presented to you. If you keep at it long enough, you will finish shaving the head. Pay careful attention not to remove the eyelashes. Remove beards on does. On bucks, the beard stays.

4. Shave the legs and feet of the goat with the #10 blade. Be sure to clip behind the dew claw and between the toes of the hoof. You may save the legs of the animal until the day of the show/event if you wish.

5. Clip the udder with a #50 blade. It's easiest to clip the udder when it is full. You may also use the #50 blade to shave just past the foreudder to accentuate the smoothness of blending there. Many people also clip the escutcheon with a #50 blade to give the illusion of a higher rear udder arch.

6. Trim the hooves and dewclaws. Use a sharp pair of scissors to clean up any stray hairs between the toes and along the coronary band.

7. When you are finished, brush the goat with a soft bristle brush to clear the hairs away. You can also bathe them again, if desired, to clear away the cut hairs and to further clean the skin. To finish, use a conditioning spray to moisturize the skin.

Dairy Cuts for Show

A dairy cut is also known as the "fuzzy show" cut. Some shows take place when it's a little too chilly for a full show cut, so we use a dairy cut to clean up the goat without sacrificing the insulation of the coat in chilly weather. When doing a dairy cut, simply trim back the fringy hair to create a sleeker, cleaner look. The easiest way to remove fringe is to use a clipper blade along the fringe very gently going WITH the grain of the hair. This should knock off most of the extra-long hairs that is affecting the silhouette of your goat.

Focus the bulk of your contouring on the backs of the legs and along the backs of the thighs, especially near the udder or, on dry does, where the udder would be. You can shave up the backs of the legs and around the escutcheon with a #7 or a #10 blade. Clean the fringe on either side of the tail and square the tip to make a tail fringe. Make sure the shaggy hair around the teats of young kids is also removed. This will accentuate the most important part of a dairy goat. If the doe is in milk, make sure to still shave the udder close, and remove any fringy hair that would obstruct the view of the udder and its attachments. You can also shave the foreudder close and gently blend the long hair of the barrel away from that area. Be sure to remove beards on does. Trim hooves and polish dew claws, and then give your goat a thorough brushing.

About Shows

Official shows are sanctioned by breed registry associations. Most shows are organized by goat clubs or local associations. The purpose of a show is to invite judges to sort goats in classes of similarly aged goats, and place them in such an order so that the first is better than the second, which is better than the third and so on. The judge uses a scorecard to compare goats to breed standards, and gives his reasons for the placings. The top goat in each age class competes for the breed Champion, and a Reserve Champion is also chosen. Later, the champion of each breed competes for Best in Show. There may be other awards a goat can win at a show that hosts a Specialty Show, including Best Udder, Best Three Does, Get of Sire, Dam and Daughter, etc.

A show is simply a judge's opinion at the time the goats are presented, so you should not place too much emphasis on winning. Shows are primarily learning experiences, and they can help you decide the direction of your breeding program, and also to understand the strengths and weaknesses of your animals when compared to other goats. Shows are also FUN! Sometimes there are fun events and auctions to participate in and it gives you a good chance to connect with other goat breeders and learn from them.

To learn more about shows for your breed of goat, go to the website of your breed association and read up on how their shows are structured. You might also find a listing of official shows to participate in. If you cannot find a list of shows, you might do a search for show discussion groups on Facebook and connect with pages that keep track of available shows.

BREEDING

Pre-Breeding

Before you begin breeding, it is important that you evaluate each doe's health and readiness. Below is a checklist that you should go through for each doe before breeding her.

Is she old enough? I like to wait until my does are eleven months old before breeding them for the first time. I also wait until they no longer look like a baby in the face, and look more like a young grown up doe. The optimum time for a doe to kid for the first time, for me, is when they are a year and a half old.

- Does she weigh enough? I raise Nigerian Dwarfs and I wait until the doe is at least 40 lbs before breeding her. Standard breeds should weigh at least 80 lbs before breeding.
- Is her coat soft and shiny and her skin free of flakes? A dull, course coat can be a sign of a mineral deficiency. Most often, it is caused by a copper deficiency. Give a copper bolus prior to breeding. Flaky skin can be a sign of mites or a sign of zinc deficiency. Figure out which one it is and solve the problem prior to breeding.
- Is she in good condition? Evaluate her body condition score prior to breeding. She should have good fleshing and should not be too thin or too fat. Yearlings have a tendency to gain excess flesh. Sometimes that can lead to difficulties conceiving, but I tend to like does to be just slightly over conditioned before I breed them so that they have plenty of fat stores for the babies to grow big and healthy. They always milk off any excess flesh once they kid.
- Is she free of internal parasites? Check her FAMACHA score and deworm if necessary. I do not like to deworm a bred doe unless I absolutely have to, so get all parasites under control before you breed.

- Is it a good time to breed? Some breeds come into estrus all year long, including minis. Other breeds only come into estrus seasonally (August-January). During the breeding season, goats will come into estrus approximately every 21 days. A goats gestation is approximately five months (145 days for minis, 150 days for standard breeds). July and August kiddings are especially rough, in my opinion. It's just too hot and controlling parasites in babies is especially difficult in the summer. Use a gestational calculator to check that the doe's due date does not interfere with important dates and holidays, and that it is a good time for you. Better yet, buy a The Goat Chick Gestational Calendar on **www.thegoatchick.com** to keep track of your due dates.
- When will she cycle next? If you will be hand breeding (explained below) then it is a good idea to start tracking your does cycles. Knowing when to expect your does next estrus cycle will make it easier for you to plan when to breed her, and in turn, when she is likely to kid if she settles.

Signs of Estrus (Heat)

Some does show all signs of heat, others show almost none. Try to pay attention to when your doe comes into heat so that you can recognize the signs that she shows. A doe is in estrus for up to 72 hours. During the first part of a doe's estrus, a buck will be interested and she may act interested, but she will not stand to let him breed her. Don't get discouraged if they do not mate on the first try. You must wait for a doe to come into standing heat, usually on the second day, and she will then allow the buck to breed her. As her standing heat wanes, the doe will not let a buck breed her again, and so you must wait for her next cycle if the mating is unsuccessful.

- Wagging tail (flagging)
- Increased vocalizations

- Sticky discharge
- Acts "bucky" (flehmen response, mounts other does, allows does to mount her)
- Change in personality
- Urinates often

Methods of Breeding

Hand Breeding- The doe and the chosen buck are put together in a private area when standing heat is observed. The handler watches the pair breed several times and then the doe and buck are returned to their normal areas.
Advantages: You will know the exact due date of the doe.
Disadvantages: Requires diligent observance of the does heat cycle.

Pen Breeding- The doe or does are put in a pen or enclosed area with one buck for approximately two months (2-3 heat cycles)
Advantages: You do not have to track does heat cycles.
Disadvantages: You will not likely know the does exact due date, only the range.

Pasture Breeding- The doe or does are put out to pasture with several bucks for approximately two months (2-3 heat cycles). A breeding harness with a unique chalk color for each buck can be provided. Breeding harnesses make a chalk mark on the back of the doe when she is bred.
Advantages: More bucks = better chances that the doe will settle.
Disadvantages: You will not likely know the does exact due date, only the range. Even with the breeding harness, it would be nearly impossible to know who bred each doe with 100% certainty without a DNA test. If you are not breeding registered animals, this may be a good option for you. Should you need to do a DNA test to determine parentage, they run about $30 each animal you have DNA typed.

Artificial Insemination (AI)- Artificial insemination is a tricky process that takes a skilled operator. Even if everything goes as planned, a doe may not settle (become pregnant) via AI for a multitude of reasons.

Advantages: You don't really need to keep a buck. You can breed your does to deceased bucks.

Disadvantages: AI is expensive, and requires alot of specialized equipment as well as a stockpile of frozen semen. Semen tanks require regular filling to keep the semen frozen. AI has a low success rate. ADGA requires that DNA be on file for all bucks collected (semen).

Doing the Deed

Goat sex lasts only a few seconds. I hand breed my does, so I usually observe all matings on my farm. When a doe is in standing heat, she will allow the buck to mount and breed her. The buck will usually attempt to woo her before he breeds her. This will be loud and messy. The buck will likely pee all over his face, in his mouth, on his beard and all over the barn, and your feet if you stand too close. He will likely sniff her vulva and often will display the Flehmen response as he inhales her scent deeply. He will stomp his feet and make all sorts of ungodly noises as he blubbers and snorts after her to woo her. Eventually, he will position himself beside her and make the leap onto her back. If she stands still for him, the mating happens quickly as he thrust himself forward sharply when he ejaculates. She, in turn, will drastically arch her back causing her spine to hump up towards the sky and her pelvis to turn sharply downwards toward the floor. This is a successful mating. She often urinates shortly after mating, expelling some of the semen so you can be sure the semen was correctly placed. I let them breed at least three times before I put them back in their normal areas.

Even if the mating is successful, that does not necessarily mean that the doe settled, or became pregnant. You should watch the doe closely for the next several days. Sometimes, a doe "short cycles" and comes back into standing heat in 5-7 days. If this happens, she should be bred again and you should write down both dates on your calendar, although the second date is most likely the "real" due date. Count ahead 21 days from the last breeding date and if she does not come back into estrus, she has likely settled.

Ways to Confirm Pregnancy

Blood Test- At thirty days bred, you can draw your doe's blood and send it off for pregnancy testing. There are several labs that do the test including SageAgLab and BioTracking. The labs will even perform CAE, CL and Johnes testing on the sample you pull, making it a great time to get it all done.

Urine Test- There is a new test on the market that is made to test the urine of cows for pregnancy. Emlab Genetics has developed the affordable P-Test. Results on goats have been mixed. I have used it before and it was accurate, but I have heard from other breeders that they do not trust the results. If you would like to give it a try, you should first decide how you will collect urine from your doe. That's the trickiest part of the test.

Ultrasound- You can ultrasound your doe to see if she has settled. The procedure should be done between 30-45 days after breeding. Waiting much longer than that will result in the inability to clearly see the amniotic sacs of the babies. I just had my herd ultrasounded for the first time this year and it is WONDERFUL!

Fetal Doppler- I have a fetal doppler, but I have never been able to use it to hear the heartbeats of kids inside their dam. It is very difficult to hear heartbeats over the rumen sounds of the dam. They are inexpensive, so it might be worth the effort to give it a try, and at least it's fun!

PregTone- The PregTone is similar to the doppler, but instead of heartbeats, it measures the presence of amniotic fluid via ultrasonic waves when held to the belly of the doe. The PregTone unit is quite expensive, though not as expensive as an ultrasound machine.

Palpating the Uterus- When the doe hits 90 days bred, you should be able to feel babies kicking in her belly. This is the method of pregnancy confirmation that I use because it does not cost anything and its very reliable. The downside is that I have to wait until the doe is 2 months from kidding, and if she is not bred I have lost valuable time to get her rebred. To use this method, put your doe in a stanchion and feed her to keep her occupied. Stand behind the doe and reach around her belly with both hands. Lay your palms flat against her belly right in front of her foreudder and pull up just slightly towards her spine. If you stay quiet and still, you should soon feel babies kicking your hands.

Just wait- You can always just wait to see if she kids on her due date. That doesn't sound like much fun, now does it?

Visual Signs of Pregnancy

Growing Belly- You may see signs of the doe "showing" her pregnancy in the last two months of pregnancy, but just like humans, does carry their babies in different ways. I've had some does who get really big very quickly, and others who you can barely tell are pregnant.

Growing Udder- This is highly variable as well. Some does show a little pouch of udder tissue early on and it continues to grow throughout the pregnancy. Others do not show much of an udder until the last few days of their gestation. Do not be alarmed if your pregnant doe is not showing an udder. The milk will come.

Vulva Changes- As the doe's pregnancy progresses, her vulva will get "puffy" and pink. You may also see some signs of discharge in the last couple of weeks. This is her body preparing for kidding and is completely normal.

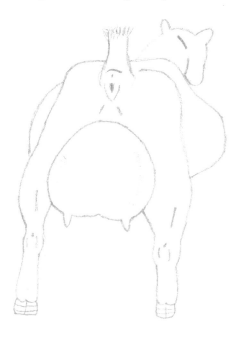

Maintenance During Pregnancy

Feed- Pregnant does need extra feed to grow healthy babies, especially in the last two months of pregnancy. Remember to make any changes in feed gradually. For more info on the nutritional requirements of pregnant does, see the Feeding section.

Hooves- Hooves grow very rapidly when a doe is pregnant. Trim her hooves every 3-4 weeks in early pregnancy. Do not trim her hooves in the last 4-6 weeks of pregnancy as the pressure on her belly makes lifting her hooves very uncomfortable.

Parasites- At my farm, I do not deworm pregnant does unless absolutely necessary. Pay attention to her FAMACHA score during her pregnancy. If you do have to deworm her, use a pregnancy safe dewormer like Ivermectin. If her FAMACHA score continues to fall, you may use Cydectin, but be aware that there is a small risk of birth defects if used early in pregnancy when the kid's skeletons are still forming. Also, be aware that you should be giving your doe a hefty dose of dewormer the day after she kids whether she is showing symptoms or not. The hormones generated during kidding may cause any internal parasites to "bloom" and overcome her weakened immune system. ALWAYS deworm a doe right after she kids.

Vitamins and Minerals- Be sure that your doe receives enough Calcium throughout her pregnancy. Daily requirement for an open (unbred) doe is 7.1g just for maintenance. Pregnant does need slightly higher daily values due to the fact they are growing little skeletons inside them. I've been known to feed a TUMS or two throughout pregnancies and especially during labor if things are moving along slowly. See the Diseases and Disorders section to learn more about the signs and symptoms of hypocalcemia. I also give a maintenance dose of BoSe (Selenium) during the final 2-4 weeks of pregnancy in order to ensure that the babies are born strong.

Vaccinations- If you have chosen to vaccinate, your doe should get a full dose of CD&T 2 weeks prior to kidding. Prepping for Labor- Several days before the does due date, I usually clean up her hind end, tail, and down the backs of her legs with a #10 blade. Kidding is a messy business, and removing the hair makes it much easier to clean her up after she kids.

PLANNING MATINGS

Choosing a buck to breed to your doe can be a complicated process. If you are serious about breeding to improve the breed you have chosen, you must select and plan matings accordingly. I must admit, many times when I choose a buck to breed to a doe it's a total crap shoot. Sometimes it works out and sometimes it doesn't. Here are some tips to help you decide on a buck to mate to your doe(s).

1. The first thing to consider when choosing a buck for your doe is to remember that you should breed for what you like. Within every breed there is bound to be different styles and types. If the current trend is to breed long, sleek does, but you happen to like short, squatty does, then by all means, go ahead and breed for it. If you do not like flashy, moonspotted bucks with blue eyes, then go ahead and breed for plain ones, and vice versa. You are the one who has to be happy with what you see when you go to the barn, so serve yourself and your interests first.

2. Evaluate your does and learn their strengths and weaknesses. You can learn more about your does by doing research, participating in goat shows, having them officially evaluated against the breed standard (i.e. Linear Appraisal), participating in production testing programs (DHI), and by asking for the honest opinions of more seasoned breeders.

3. Be patient. Changing a trait or characteristic in your herd TAKES A LONG TIME! To fully evaluate a doe takes approximately 2.3-3 years from her birth, or until she freshens for the second time. Don't get too caught up in making huge changes quickly. In fact, focus on just one or two traits you would like to improve per season.

4. When you find a potential buck to breed to your does, take a look at his dam and his freshened daughters. His female relatives are the biggest indicator of what the buck is likely to produce. Many very successful breeders buy bucks sight unseen, and rely solely on pedigrees and production data from him and his female relatives. You should also consider the information contained in his pedigree and the production and linear data available on him and his relatives from your breed registry. We will talk more about Understanding Pedigrees later.

5. Hope for the best. If a breeding doesn't pan out the way you planned, try, try again.

KIDDING

Kidding season is a joyous time, but it can also be frustrating, stressful, and heartbreaking. To set the tone for this magical time, I republish the following poem "Doe Code of Honor" below. Every goat breeder knows the Code and every doe lives by it. It should tell you everything you need to know about this special time.

Doe Code of Honor

The doe's secret code of honor is as old as goats themselves and is the species best kept secret. No doe shall ever kid before its time. (Its time being determined by the following factors):

1- No kid shall be born until total chaos has been reached by all involved. Your owner's house must be a wreck, their family hungry and desperate for clean clothes, and their social life nonexistent.

2- "Midwives" must reach the babbling fool status before you kid out. Bloodshot eyes, tangled hair and the inability to form a sentence mean the time is getting close.

3- For every bell, beeper, camera or whistle they attach to you, kidding must be delayed by at least one day for each item. If they use an audio monitor, one good yell per hour will keep things interesting.

4- If you hear the words, "She's nowhere near ready. She'll be fine while we're away for the weekend," Wait until they load the car, then begin pushing!

5- Owner stress must be at an all time high! If you are in the care of someone else, ten to fifteen phone calls a day is a sign you're getting close.

6- When you hear the words "I can't take it anymore!" wait at least three more days.

7 -You must keep this waiting game interesting. False alarms are mandatory! Little teasers such as looking at your stomach, pushing your food around in the bucket and then walking away from it, and nesting, are always good for a rise. Be creative and find new things to do to keep the adrenaline pumping in those who wait.

8- The honor of all goats is now in your hands. Use this time to avenge all of your barn mates. Think about your friend who had to wear that silly costume in front of those people. Hang onto that baby for another day. OH, they made him do tricks too! Three more days seems fair. Late feedings, the dreaded diet, bad haircuts, those awful wormings can also be avenged at this time.

9- If you have fulfilled all of the above and are still not sure when to have the kids, listen to the weather forecast on the radio that has been so generously provided by those who wait. Severe storm warning is what you're waiting for. In the heart of the storm jump into action! The power could go out and you could have the last laugh. You have a good chance of those who wait missing the whole thing while searching for a flashlight that works!

10- Make the most of your interrupted nights. Beg for food each time someone comes into the barn to check you. Your barn mates will love you as the extra goodies fall their way too.

Remember, this code of honor was designed to remind man of how truly special goats are. Do your best to reward those who wait with a beautiful doeling to carry on the Doe Code of Honor for the next generation of those who wait.

Author Unknown

Signs of Labor

Just like the signs of estrus discussed in the previous section, a doe may display all signs of labor or only a few.

- Loosening of the broad sacrotuberous ligament*
- Tight, shiny, full udder*
- Seeks solitude*
- Hollowing near the thurls
- White mucus discharge
- Tail raises with contractions
- May stop eating (this has never happened on my farm)
- Stargazing
- Becomes restless
- Becomes vocal
- Paws the ground
- Licking her lips or the air
- Nibbling at her sides

*The most important items above that will PREDICT labor are the first three. As such, I will further describe those items below.

The very BEST way to predict when a doe will kid is to pay attention to two specific areas of her body. The udder, and her broad sacratuberous ligaments. As labor approaches, the ligaments to either side of her tail will slacken. The ligaments will get looser until you cannot feel them anymore. When this happens, and the udder fills and gets tight, labor will start within the next several hours.

As labor nears, the doe will seek solitude away from the rest of the herd. She will look around for a safe space to have her babies where she won't be bothered by other goats. As solitude is observed, move the doe to the spot where you want her to have her babies (i.e. a kidding stall) because labor is imminent.

TO DO: Check ligaments and udder texture several times per day starting a day or two before her due date until she kids. Feel for two narrow pencil-like structures on either side of the tail, behind the thurls to either side of the tail towards the pins. When the doe is unbred or is not ready to kid they will be stiff like two angled thin pencils. Push down to feel them under your fingers.

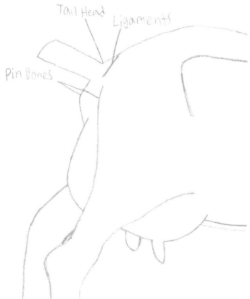

It takes some practice to find the right location, but once you finally feel them, you will never forget where they should be. Try feeling them on your goat now to practice, so that when they are close to kidding you will know where they are.

Kidding Supplies

- Vet Emergency Number
- Your Mentor's Number
- Old Towels
- Absorbent (Puppy) Pads
- Lubricant
- Surgical Gloves
- Bulb Aspirator
- Piglet (or Lamb) OB Snare
- Iodine
- Surgical Scissors
- Nutridrench or Molasses
- A Big Bucket
- Tube Feeding Kit
- A Hair Dryer
- Insulin Needles
- BoSe Injectible
- Vit B Complex
- Dexamethizone
- Adrenaline (Epinephrine)

Important Note:
TAKE YOUR RINGS OFF WHEN YOUR DOE GOES INTO LABOR!

The Labor Process- Stage One

During the first stage of labor, the does uterus contracts to open her cervix to allow her kids to be born. This early stage of labor can last several hours. The biggest factor that affects the length of this first stage of labor is the position of the first kid. If the first kid is positioned correctly, his nose and feet will press against the cervix and cause it to open more efficiently. If the kid is not positioned correctly, then this stage of labor could be delayed. As you get more experienced with assisting at kiddings, you will be able to tell with some amount of certainty if the first kid is not positioned correctly due to how long the doe has been in labor. I usually let the doe contract for a couple of hours, and then go in to check the position of the kid and check her cervix. More on that later.

During this stage your doe may act restless, be vocal, paw the ground, exhibit the Flehmen response, and back her hind end up into a corner with strong contractions. Her mucus discharge will go from white, to clear and stringy, and then finally to yellow and ropey. Her tail will raise up with each contraction. Just like in humans, her contractions should get gradually stronger and closer together. As she progresses, she will eventually start to lie down with strong contractions. She will also normally kick her legs out straight from her body and hold them there as her contraction continues. This is the sign that the second stage of labor is starting and she is ready to push.

Please be aware that some goats like to push in a squatting position, so do not completely rely on her laying down and kicking her legs out to observe pushing. I've had goats deliver completely standing up before, and when they push they squat as if to urinate.

The Labor Process- Stage Two
Stage Two begins when the doe starts to push. This is also known as active labor. She might start off with a few test pushes just to see how it feels. She will most likely be lying down (although I've had a few deliver while standing) with her legs stretched out stiffly from her body. She may also brace herself against a wall, a fence or the floor to get more traction. If you have a walled stall, 9 times out of 10 the doe will position her butt in a corner where you can't see. This is ok as she will likely get up and down again many times before the first kid is born. She may begin licking the air and licking your hands as the hormones surge through her body in preparation for her to clean up her newborn kids.

Pushing can be identified by the raising up of the hind end in short bursts. She may grunt as she pushes. You may not see much progress at first, especially if she is a first freshener. If you have not seen any progress in 30 minutes of pushing, it is time to go in and feel for the presentation of the first kid. More on that later. The second stage of labor ends when the last kid is born.

As kids are born, clear their mouths and noses immediately with a towel. When they are breathing well, move them to the dam's head so that she can clean them up while you wait for the next kid to be born. ALWAYS ASSUME THAT THERE ARE MORE KIDS IN THERE! I never leave a doe alone until she passes her placenta and I know that she is finished. We will further explore how to care for kids once they are born in the Kid Care section.

Stages of Labor- Stage Three

During the third stage of labor, the kids have been born and momma is busy licking them clean. The passing of the placenta is the third stage. After the kids are born, you may see some bloody cordlike tissue and fluid filled bubbles hanging out of the doe's vulva. This is the placenta, and your doe should deliver it naturally about 45-60 minutes after the last kid is born. DO NOT PULL THE PLACENTA! When it is delivered, you can allow the doe to eat it so that she can replenish her body with the nutrients it contains, or you can clear it away.

If the placenta has not been delivered within two hours of the kids being born, it is possible that your doe has a retained placenta, although a true retained placenta is one that has not been passed in 12 hours. This is usually the sign of something else, most likely selenium deficiency. In a true retained placenta, your vet will probably prescribe oxytocin to induce the delivery of the placenta. You must be absolutely sure that the doe's cervix is still open when using oxytocin. Natural oxytocin can be generated in the doe's body by simply milking the doe.

Care After Delivery
The day following delivery, give your doe a full spa treatment. Clean up her hind end by giving her a sponge bath. Brush out her coat. Clip her udder short so that the babies can readily nurse. Milk out some of her colostrum to freeze and use in an emergency. Give her hooves a good trimming, and DEWORM WITH CYDECTIN! Deworming after kidding is extremely important, because the hormones generated by labor and delivery can cause a massive barberpole bloom, which can overwhelm a doe very quickly, causing death.

KIDDING ISSUES (DYSTOCIA)

Kidding Issues or Difficult Birth is called dystocia. We will not be talking here about the causes of dystocia, we will only be presenting the specific situations and how to solve the issue.

Checking The Cervix
If the doe has been in labor for a long time with no visible progress, it is advisable that you enter the doe to see what's going on.

1. Use surgical gloves and lube to enter the doe.
2. Move slowly and carefully and push your index and middle fingers into the doe. The cervix lies approximately four inches from the vaginal opening, and slightly down towards the barrel of the doe. If you have short fingers you may have to push further than you think.
3. Sweep your fingers in a circular motion around the walls of the vagina at the depth of a cervix. You should feel the open or partially open cervix at the tip of your fingers. The opening of the cervix feels thin but strong, and circular. When the cervix is completely open, you should be able to feel the edges of it along the walls of the vagina. If it is not fully open, you will be able to feel the size of the opening.
4. If you push a little farther, you should be able to feel a kid or a bag of waters beyond the cervix, but if the cervix is not yet fully dilated then don't worry if you can't yet feel a kid behind it. Let her labor longer until her cervix is completely ready.

Incomplete Dilation of the Cervix

A rare complication that occurs is incomplete dilation of the cervix, also known as ring womb. If the cervix is partially open, you can gently encourage the dilation by very gently rimming around the opening of the cervix. Wait some time, and then check her again to see if the cervix has dilated more. You can also give lutalyse to encourage the cervix to open if she is not progressing. In some cases, the cervix will not progress or will not open normally. In this instance, you must call your vet to intervene. The vet may prescribe drugs to encourage the cervix to open, or in extreme cases, he may recommend a cesarean section. NEVER try to force the cervix to open as you will likely cause irreparable damage and scar tissue that will cause problems for later kiddings.

Presentations

When you check for presentation of a kid, go slowly and calmly into the doe with your entire hand. Don't forget the lube! The womb is positioned well below the opening of the vagina, so you are going to go inside and then immediately down towards the barrel of the doe. You might feel confused about what you are feeling. Close your eyes and try to visualize what the kid looks like and try to identify the specific parts of the kid. The muzzle can be identified by feeling for the bottom teeth of the kid. This will also tell you which way the head is positioned. Teeth should be on the bottom, since goats do not have top teeth. If you have to sort out legs, feel the feet and determine which way the pasterns are bending. That will help you identify whether you have ahold of a back or a front leg. When pulling a kid, be sure that you pull towards the doe's feet in a curved motion, and not straight out. Doing so could injure the doe and the kid. NEVER EVER PULL A KID IF THE DOE IS NOT PUSHING! ONLY PULL WITH THE DOE'S CONTRACTIONS/PUSHES!

Presentation Positions

Four Legs and Head
A kid cannot be born in this position. You must push the back legs back down into the womb until the front legs and head only are presenting.

Front Legs Presenting, Head Back
A kid cannot be born in this position. Place your hand into the doe above the front legs and let your hand travel in a downward direction to find the head and pull it up towards the birth canal. You may have to use a snare to retrieve the head, especially if the kid is not alive.

Normal Anterior Presentation
This is the normal presentation of a kid. His front legs and head are positioned in the birth canal. A doe should not need any help with this presentation unless the kid is large.

Posterior Presentation, Single Leg A kid cannot be born in this position. You must enter the doe and retrieve the leg that is down. Once you have both legs, you can pull them together and deliver the kid. You must pull smoothly and quickly with all posterior positions, because the umbilical cord will break before the kid's head is delivered, causing the kid to take a breath inside. This presentation is similar to a full posterior presentation, with the butt only presenting. In this case, you must retrieve both rear legs before pulling.

Breech Presentation
In most cases, this presentation is quite normal and the kid can be delivered in this position. You must pull smoothly and quickly with all posterior positions, because the umbilical cord will break before the kid's head is delivered, causing the kid to take a breath inside, and aspirate fluid.

Upside Down A kid cannot be born in this position. This is one of the toughest presentations to correct, but luckily it is very rare. The kid needs to be flipped over so that the head and front feet are presenting in a normal presentation, instead of upside down. The easiest way to correct this is to bend the front legs close to the kid's body, get ahold of the head, and twist 180 degrees while you bring the head up towards the birth canal. You may need a snare.

Spine First A kid cannot be born in this position. This is another difficult presentation to correct. If the spine is presenting first, you need to careful enter the doe and push the kid away from the birth canal and find the head. It takes quite a bit of maneuvering to get the kid into position to be delivered. Just move slowly and you can grab the head and pull and twist him up into position. Do not worry about the front legs. Find the head and pull it up into position to be born. It is possible that you may need to use a snare to correct this position, but you have to push the kid back down to get to the head.

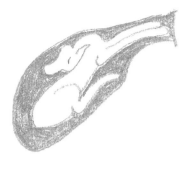

Head Upside Down and Back A kid cannot be born in this position. This position is similar to Front Legs Presenting, Head Back but the head is actually backwards and upside down. To correct this position you need to push the kid back down into the womb to make room to flip the head over. Once you have the head flipped, the kid can be delivered normal. This position, however, is bound to have a high mortality rate, especially if the doe has been pushing for a long time with the kids head backwards and upside down.

Backwards, Back of Head First A kid cannot be born in this position. This position looks pretty serious but you should be able to enter the doe and grab ahold of the head and twist slowly so that the head enters the birth canal normally. The body should follow the head in a normal presentation position. Just twist and pull slowly.

Head Down A kid cannot be born in this position. This position is fairly easy to correct. Enter the doe and sweep your fingers down and around to catch the muzzle of the kid and pull it up into the birth canal. If the kid is large, you may need to push the front legs back down to release some pressure in order to free the head enough to lift the muzzle to the birth canal. Make sure that the head is raised up enough so that it lays on top of the front legs. I once had a kid try to come out with one leg over his head and I had a very difficult time moving the leg back down to where it belonged because the kid was large.

Presentation of Multiples

Multiples are common in most breeds. Sometimes, two kids try to come out at the same time. causing legs from different kids to enter the birth canal. You must move slowly but deliberately to untangle the kids. Try to identify which legs belong to which kids by following the legs to the body. Don't be afraid to gently push one kid back down into the womb so that it is out of the way of the first to be born. In extreme cases, you may have to use a snare to hold one kids head while you push the other back down into the womb.

Kid Too Large to Deliver

In the case that a kid is too large to deliver, call your vet immediately. Do not delay. The doe may need a cesarean section to deliver the kid.

Hemorrhaging

If the doe is bleeding an excess of bright red blood after she delivers, she may be hemorrhaging. Check the color of your doe's eye membranes and gums, and make sure they stay pink. If they are pale, you may be in a very bad situation. Call your vet immediately, as it could be a sign of a ruptured uterus or a torn cervix, which are both extremely serious situations. Sometimes you can stop the bleeding with oxytocin, as the drug causes the uterus to clamp down and stop the hemorrhaging. Other times, when the hemorrhaging is serious and cannot be stopped, your doe will bleed out and die in 24-72 hours. I lost a doe due after kidding due to uterine tear in January 2018. It was absolutely heartbreaking. I lost the doe and all three of her kids. She slowly bled out and died 28 hours after she kidded.

Torsion of the Uterus

Torsion, or twisting, of the uterus is quite rare, but it can happen. The uterus can get twisted, trapping the kids inside the womb. There are some really interesting videos on YouTube which show the process to correct torsion of the uterus. I, an experienced breeder, would not feel comfortable intervening in this matter so I recommend vet intervention in order to very careful untwist the uterus so that the kids can be born.

After Dystocia

In most cases, when you have had to enter a doe and manipulate kids to help deliver them, you should start the doe on a round of antibiotics in order to stave off any infection you may have introduced. Oxytetracycline is the preferred antibiotic for reproductive issues, and you can administer the first dose directly into the uterus with a syringe (no needle) through the cervix, after the placenta is delivered.

A doe's vulva may be swollen after dystocia, or after serious manipulation of kids. After the placenta is delivered, use warm soapy water to clean her up, and apply hemorrhoid cream to her vulva to reduce the swelling. A doe will normally have a bloody discharge for up to two weeks after delivery as her uterus is cleaned out naturally. If her discharge turns foul smelling, she likely has an infection and you should start antibiotics right away.

KID CARE

Kid Care at Birth

1. Make sure the kid is breathing.

Clear the nose and mouth of birthing fluids with a towel first. If the kid is breathing, but the breath is rattling, use a bulb aspirator to clear the nose and mouth of fluids. If the breath is still rattling, you can hold the kid upside down and gently sling the fluids out of them towards the ground. This maneuver takes some practice. Be sure to have a good grip on the kid before you sling him.

If the kid is NOT breathing, clear the mouth and nose, sling the kid and recheck for breaths. Vigorously rub the kid with a towel to encourage breathing. If the kid is still NOT breathing, check for a heartbeat by putting the kids barrel to your ear. If a heartbeat is not present, you can compress the chest by putting your thumb on one side of the chest and your fingers on the other side of the chest and gently squeezing to encourage the heart to beat. You can also give the kid gentle breaths by covering the nose and the mouth with your mouth and give a very soft puff of air. In a last ditch attempt, you can give a dose of epinephrine with an insulin needle under the kids tongue to stimulate him to life. If all efforts fail, the kid is dead.

When the kid is revived and starts to breathe and his heart is beating, continue to rub him vigorously with towels and then proceed to the next tip below. Recheck his vitals and make sure his lungs are clear and his heartbeat is strong. He is probably going to need alot of care from this point forward, but it IS possible for him to make a full recovery.

2. Make sure the kid has normal body temperature.

The second most important issue to worry about is not food, it is body temperature. A cold kid (<100° F) will not eat, so that makes it more important than food for a newborn. Body temperature really has nothing to do with the temperature of a barn, and it can be 80 degrees room temp and the kid can still die from hypothermia if he cannot regulate his own body temperature. The easiest way to tell if your kid has a normal temperature is to stick your CLEAN index finger in his mouth. His tongue and mouth should feel warm. If his tongue feels cool, then he has a subnormal temperature, and you must act quickly to correct it. This is what the big bucket is for. Fill your bucket with warm water (103°-104° F). Lower the kid into the bucket so that the waterline is at his neck, and hold him there for fifteen minutes. Don't worry, he will not struggle and will probably fall asleep as he assumes he is back in the womb. After you remove him from the bucket, towel dry him and use a hair dryer to dry his hair. Be careful that you do not burn him with the hair dryer. After you get his body temperature normal, you may proceed to the 3rd step, but be aware that you need to keep a close eye on him and if his body temperature drops again, you will need to give him another hot bath until his body begins to regulate his temperature on its own.

3. Make sure the kid gets colostrum

Colostrum is the kids first milk. After a doe freshens, her first milk is slightly yellow and very thick. This is colostrum, and it is as good as gold to the goat breeder, and to the kids. It is packed full of vitamins and immunizes the kid against many threats. You should always use natural colostrum, and only use a replacer if you absolutely have to. You can freeze colostrum in small bags and keep them in the freezer in case of emergency.

If you do not have colostrum because the doe did not produce, you may be able to call local goat producers to buy some. By the time the kid is dry, and starts to stand and walk (usually within the first ten minutes after birth) he will start rooting around for a teat. The dam will push him back towards her udder to encourage him to eat. Strip the does teats by giving them each a squeeze. This will clear away the natural plugs that have been keeping her colostrum safe inside her udder. Some kids find the teat right away, while others have to be encouraged and guided there. I never leave the barn before every kid has a full belly.

If you are going to bottle raise the kids, milk the colostrum out of the dam, warm it, and bottle feed it to the kids. It is not recommended to use a microwave to warm colostrum, but use hot water to warm the bottle instead.

4. Make sure his umbilical cord has been dipped in iodine
Use a strong iodine dip to coat the umbilical to the belly. You can trim the umbilical with clean surgical scissors if they are too long. Iodine will seal out bacteria and guard against the kid getting naval ill. You can also iodine the hooves if you wish.

Problems with Newborn Kids

Kid Will Not Stand- Some kids take longer than others to stand up and start walking. Smaller kids generally have a harder time getting going than larger kids. If the kid is having trouble standing or stands up but keeps falling down, he might be selenium deficient. If a kid tries to stand and walk but cannot after 30 minutes, give him 1/4cc of BoSe subQ with an insulin needle behind his front leg or give him oral selenium gel as directed on the tube. Remove the kid from his dam and siblings immediately until he gains strength. You might also give him some warm black coffee or molasses to give him some energy.

Kid Will Not Eat- Check his body temperature by putting your index finger in his mouth. If it is cool, he needs a hot bath to bring his body temperature up to normal. If his temperature is normal (warm) then he might be developmentally delayed and has not yet developed the suck reflex. This happens alot with smaller kids (runts) and bucks. If he will not latch onto his dam's teat, express a little colostrum into a pop bottle and warm it up under hot running water. Attach a Pritchard nipple and see if he will take a little colostrum from the bottle. If he hasn't taken any colostrum within the first two hours of birth, it's time to start thinking about tubing him (explained below).

Kid Has Not Pooped- A newborns first poop is called meconium, and it is dark, sticky and tar-like. Kids should pass their meconium within the first few hours. Once they start eating, their little bodies will start working and things will start moving through them. I am always quick to give newborn babies a warm, soapy enema if they are having any issues, because I really think it kickstarts their bodies to start working like they should. Poop will soon turn yellow and sticky as the colostrum moves through them. It will stay yellow and sticky for several weeks.

Kid is Down- If a kid is down, you have a serious issue. Kids who act depressed, won't eat, won't stand, and won't make an effort to do so is in serious trouble. If a kid is down, remove him from his dam and siblings immediately. He should be brought into the house where you can care for him properly. I use a large plastic tote that I line with a towel, and hook up a small heating pad under the towel. This becomes my NICU incubator that I keep next to my bed. You have three major things to worry about when a kid is in the NICU. He needs warmth, nutrition and he needs to be eliminating waste. If he cannot keep his temperature up, continue to give him hot baths. Try to bottle him as soon as he is warm. If he will not eat, he needs to be tubed. Give him a soapy enema to stimulate his bowels to move. You can start giving him Vit B Complex and Dexamethazone to help him gain strength. You have an uphill battle with a down kid, but it is possible to pull them through. You need to keep them warm, fed and eliminating waste to get over the hill. Keep trying to get him to stand and offer him a bottle until he takes it.

How to Get a Kid to Take a Bottle

Seems so simple, but sometimes it is not. To get a kid to take a bottle, make sure that the milk is warmed to body temperature (103° F). Then you need to think like a momma goat. Think about what the dam does to encourage him to eat. She licks his behind and messes with his back end to push him towards the teat. When he gets there, he will nudge the teat and his forehead will hit his dam's belly. So, you just need to simulate those same things. Hold the kid across your lap towards your dominant hand. Hold the bottle in your dominant hand and put it in his mouth with your palm cupping underneath his chin and holding the bottle with your fingers. With your other hand, you may have to tickle his tail and his butt like his dam would do. With your chin, bend over and rub the top of his head so that he thinks he is standing under his dam. It takes practice to get this right, but this is the best way to encourage a kid to drink from a bottle.

How to Tube a Newborn Kid

Kids must eat to survive, so if the kid will not eat, you must tube nutrients into them in order for them to survive. Tubing a kid with colostrum seems scary, but it is essential that you learn how to do it. You will need a Weak-Kid Syringe and Stomach Tube. JeffersPet sells them for under $3 each.

1. Warm some colostrum under hot running water.
2. Measure the tube from the kids mouth to the last rib. This is how much tube you need to put into the kid.
3. Lay the kid down on its side.
4. Thread the tube into the kids mouth down the side of the throat. If you meet resistance, pull it out and start again. When you reach the length that you previously measured, stop.
5. Listen to the end of the tube for breath sounds. This will ensure that you are in the stomach and not in the lungs.

6. Attach the syringe and pour 1 oz of colostrum at a time into the syringe. Introduce the colostrum slowly as to not overwhelm the kids little stomach. You can lift the head to have gravity assist the liquid into the stomach. Tube a total of 2 oz of colostrum for the first feeding. This little bit of nutrition might be enough to jump start the kid to eat.
7. Pinch the tube before pulling out the tube, because liquid could enter the lungs otherwise. Make sure you keep the tube pinched until the entire tube exits the body.
8. Tube the newborn 4 times per day until he starts eating on his own.

How to Give a Kid an Enema
To give a kid a soapy water enema you will need a 6cc sliplock syringe and a short length of IV tubing.
1. Prepare a bit of warm, soapy water to use. Dish washing liquid works fine.
2. Cut a few inches of IV tubing and push it onto the sliplock syringe.
3. Draw up the soapy water into the syringe.
4. Lay the goat on a towel. This can get really messy.
5. Use a bit of the soapy water to lubricate the anus.
6. Carefully, push the tubing into the anus a few inches. BE VERY CAREFUL!
7. Slowly push some soapy water into the goat, (3cc for minis, 6cc for standards) and then withdraw the tubing.
8. I usually stand the goat up at this point and wait. There may be bubbles. There will be soapy water that either leaks or shoots out of the goat's anus. The sticky meconium will also make an exit. Catch everything with the towel and clean the goat up after he is done. Repeat as necessary to get the bowels moving.

How to Care for Healthy Kids (Birth-Weaning)

A kid's main diet from birth is milk. If you choose to dam raise, then the dam takes care of the milk. If you choose to bottle raise the kids, then give the kids as much milk as they want, four times per day from birth. A daily schedule might be: 7am, 1pm, 7pm, 1am. Whichever schedule you choose, they should be fed every six hours for the first two weeks. When they hit two weeks old, back off to three times per day. To do this, drop the last feeding so that there is 12 hours between the last feeding of the night and the first feeding in the morning. This will give the kid a bedtime and a rise time. When the kids are about a month old, you can back off their feedings to two times per day. Kids can be weaned as early as eight weeks of age, but most breeders wait to wean until they are 10-12 weeks old. Kids can have hay immediately after they are born, and some start nibbling on it at just a few days old. You can introduce grain when the kids are two weeks old, but they may not be interested in it until they are about a month old. It takes quite awhile for kids to start drinking water. Mine usually start sneaking little drinks around 6 weeks of age. You should not wean the kids until they are drinking water, and eating hay and grain readily. To wean, back their bottles down to one per day for two weeks, and then cut the other bottle the following week. Kids may be whiny for several days while they adjust to their new feeding schedule.

Kids should be disbudded as soon as horn buds can be felt. Bucks usually develop hornbuds earlier than does, sometimes at birth. We usually disbud bucks at around 3 days old, and does at 1 week. If you choose to vaccinate, kids should get their first CDT shot at 3 weeks of age, and then another booster dose at 6 weeks of age. Kids can start on a cocci prevention program (maintenence oral doses of DiMethox 12.5%) at three weeks of age.

Kids should be tattooed when they are registered. I like to wait until they are three months of age before I tattoo them, unless I absolutely have to for a show.

Although many farms recommend castrating bucks as young as four weeks of age, I WHOLEHEARTEDLY AND STRONGLY DISAGREE. I wait until the bucks are 12 weeks of age before they are castrated.

CASTRATING

Ninety-nine percent of all bucks born on our farm are castrated and sold as pets. We will talk about castrating practices in a few, but first I want to make the case for WAITING TO CASTRATE until bucklings are ready. Many farms, suggest castrating at four to six weeks of age. I have found in my experiences that castrating a buckling that early greatly increases the chance of him suffering from urinary calculi, which is a very serious and mostly incurable deadly condition.

Many believe that feeding alfalfa to bucks causes UC. That is not entirely true. Bucks and wethers require a BALANCED diet just like does do, and feeding alfalfa is not the entire issue. UC has recently become a huge problem because of the castrating practices of some breeders. In an effort to move animals out, breeders are castrating WAY too early. I've heard of some that castrate as young as three weeks of age so they can move them to their new homes quickly to lessen their workload. These wethers have an extremely high chance of dying from UC, and I have taken dozens of calls over the years asking me for help with little wethers who have developed UC. Sadly, there is usually no hope.

When you remove the testicles, testosterone production stops, which is what helps the urethra grow. The bigger the urethra at castration, the easier it is for the goat to pass stones, should they develop, through normal urination. I do not castrate before 12 weeks of age for this very reason, and I have NEVER had a single issue with UC, neither on my farm or at a wether's new home.

Methods of Castration

Whichever method of castration you choose, you should give the buckling a dose of tetanus antitoxin at the time of castration. This dose will protect him for ten days from contracting tetanus.

Banding- At our farm, we band bucklings to castrate them. The band cuts off circulation to the testicles. In a few weeks the testicles shrivel and within 6-8 weeks, the shriveled scrotum and testicles fall off with the band. For this, you will need a band elastrator, bands, and iodine. We give a full dose of banamine approximately 20 minutes before we band. The dose is 1cc per 100 lbs so we weigh the buckling and then use an insulin needle to give a subQ dose. Put the buckling in a stanchion and give him some food. Wash the testicles with iodine. Use gloves if you don't want to stain your hands. Put the green band over the elastrator and open it all the way by squeezing the elastrator with your hand. Place the testicles through the band, making sure that BOTH testicles are through the elastrator. Release your grip on the elastrator and flip the rubber band off of the elastrator one tine at a time until the band is above the testicles, close to his body. Check that his teats are not caught in the band. The buckling will not feel any pain until the pressure in his testicles build from the blood supply being cut off. The sensation is probably similar to putting a string around your finger. It takes about 15-20 minutes for him to feel it, at which point he will probably start crying and rolling around on the ground. The banamine helps ease the pain immensely, and many times, my bucklings will fall asleep during the worst of the pain, which only lasts a couple of hours. When the testicles eventually go numb, the buckling feels no more pain and will go back to his day.

Cutting- Some breeders choose to cut the scrotum and pull out the testicles. This is obviously a very effective and immediate method of castration. Honestly, I just don't have the stomach for it. The process involves having a person hold down the buckling while you make a cut across the scrotum with a scalpel. Next you pull the testicles out of the scrotum and cut the spermatic cords. I have no personal experience with this method, but some people choose this method because the results are immediate, the trauma is short, and the recovery is quick.

Burdizzo- The burdizzo is an emasculator, which is a tool that crushes the spermatic cords above the testicles. Along with banding, this is a bloodless method of castration and if done correctly, is completely effective. To perform a castration using the burdizzo, locate the spermatic cords in the scrotum. The spermatic cords should be about the size of a pencil in the upper portion of the scrotum above the testicles. Position the burdizzo over one side of the scrotum, over one of the spermatic cords. Clamp down for 10-20 seconds. Repeat on the other side. Watch the animal closely over the next few days to make sure that the castration was successful. If successful, the testicles will be reabsorbed into the body, leaving an empty scrotum.

Please note: Some 4H wether programs do not allow any sign of a scrotum in order for the child to show the wether. Do your research into which method of castration will create the most effective results by the time you take your animals to the fair.

Castration After Care
Watch the castration site for redness, swelling, bleeding and signs of infection. In case of infection, a broad-spectrum antibiotic should be administered.

HORNS, SCURS AND DISBUDDING

Horns vs. Scurs

We are not going to talk about the Horned vs Disbudded debate here. It is briefly discussed in the section Choose Your Goats.

Horns are not scurs and scurs are not horns. A horn is a naturally occurring appendage of the goat which is used for self-defense, sparring with herd members, and for helping regulate their internal body temperature. Scurs are small, rudimentary horn growths that occur sometimes after a goat is disbudded. Scurs are generally only attached to the skin, not the skull, so goats regularly cast them off by rubbing their heads on fences and by sparring with other goats. Scurs are most common in bucks, as the scurs are helped along via testosterone.

Most scurs occur in front of the hornbud, but they can occur other places. Some new goat owners mistake the scur for a horn growing back. Scurs are not horns, and they do not grow in the same place that horns would grow. Scurs are nothing to be alarmed about, and goats usually do not have them for very long. If a scur gets too long, you can band them with rubber bands and they will fall off.

Causes of scurs on does include disbudding too late, and disbudding incorrectly. Some bucks will grow scurs no matter how thorough the disbudding job was.

Disbudding a Baby Goat

Disbudding correctly takes some practice. I remember when we first started doing it, we had scurs EVERYWHERE. Baby goats should be disbudded within the first ten days of life. Bucks generally need to be disbudded earlier than doelings. When you can feel the hornbuds they are ready to disbud.

Tools Needed:
- Disbudding Iron
- Disbudding Box (optional)
- Leather Gloves
- Pocket Knife (We clean it thoroughly with alcohol just prior to the procedure)
- AluShield or Wound Kote

1. Preheat the disbudding iron for about 10 minutes. Gather the baby to be disbudded. Some people like to trim the hair around the hornbuds with an electric trimmer to make it easier to see.
2. When the iron is properly heated, secure the goat either in a disbudding box or securely in yourself or your helpers arms. Don't forget your gloves! **It's extremely important that the baby goat is not able to move.**
3. Place the iron around the hornbud of the goat. The open circle of the iron goes around the tip of the bud. Let the weight of the iron be your pressure and rotate the pressure in a counter clockwise motion for 3-4 seconds. Use 5 seconds for bucklings. You want to see a copper ring where the iron was. If you do not have a copper ring, your iron is not hot enough or you did not burn long enough. In this case, let the head cool and then try again.

4. When you see a copper ring, take your knife and cut the horn bud off. It will pop off easily. It may or may not bleed. If it does bleed, just cauterize that area with the hot iron.
5. Cool the head by blowing on it. We spray the two wounds with AluShield to seal out any bacteria, but you can also use Wound Kote or no sealant at all.

PLEASE NOTE: There are two disbudding videos on my website at **www.thegoatchick.com/horns-scurs-and-disbudding.html** *Some people disbud bucklings differently than doelings, and the videos show both. Videos are posted by permission of Helmstead Minis.*

TATTOOING A GOAT

The following is an excerpt of a 01/21/2013 blog post from my farm page. I've added some additional updated comments in italics.

At Twin Willows, as at most farms, we tattoo the ears. *(Lamanchas have very small ears so you tattoo the tail web in the same way)* The herd name designator (ours is TWF) goes in the right ear, and the year letter (preferred letter for 2012 is B, 2013 will be C, etc.) and unique number go in the left ear. Most breeders use birth order to choose the unique number. For example, if the goat you are tattooing was the first kid born in 2012, their unique code would be B1, and if they were the fifth kid born that year, the code would be B5, and so on. This letter/number combination goes in the left ear, and is unique to every goat in your herd.

Tattooing Supplies

You will need:

- Tattoo pliers (we use two)
- Green paste tattoo ink
- Letters and numbers to fit your pliers
- A toothbrush designated specifically for this job
- Rubbing alcohol
- Cotton balls
- LOTS of Paper Towels
- Surgical Gloves
- Antimicrobial Foaming Hand Wash
- Blood stop powder (Just in case. Trust me.)
- A piece of paper or thin card board (MUY IMPORTANTE'!)
- A small container for cleaning used letters/numbers

Procedure:
1. First things first, secure your goat in a stanchion and give him some grain.
2. Next, arrange the letters and/or numbers in the pliers, and screw down the set screw. It's also a good idea to set out the numbers and/or letters you will need for the next ear. Once you get the numbers and letters in place CHECK YOUR ORIENTATION ON A PIECE OF PAPER OR CARDBOARD!! This is very important. Even if you KNOW that you put them in right, CHECK ANYWAYS! The worst thing would be learning that you put a number in upside down AFTER you tattoo the ear. Next, put your gloves on and dispense some of the green ink paste onto your toothbrush. Coat the needles with the ink on the toothbrush. *Note: I have found over the years that if you coat the ear with the ink paste after you clean it, and then push the ink through the ear with the pliers, that your letters will last longer.*
3. Next, apply a liberal amount of antimicrobial foam to a cotton ball and clean the inside of the goat's ears. Use a clean cotton ball for each ear.
4. Next, position your pliers to the inside of the right ear to apply the herd designator. Be careful to position the letters/numbers to a smooth part of the ear to attempt staying away from any veins.

5. Next, take your toothbrush and scrub the ink into the wounds. Change out your letters/numbers for the next ear (or grab your other set of pliers.) Repeat the same process using the new code for the left ear. Remember, date code and unique number go in the left ear. Your goat will probably be jumpier when you start the next ear, so have someone help hold his head if he is too much to handle by yourself. After both ears are tattooed give him some love and tell him he was a good boy. I like to let them finish eating so I can watch them for a few minutes to make sure there is no bleeding. When you are finished tattooing, your pliers, letters, toothbrush and everything else that has ink on it (it always gets EVERYWHERE!) can be cleaned up with the rubbing alcohol and paper towels. I like to soak the letters in a small container of rubbing alcohol. I recommend NOT taking your gloves off until you are done cleaning. *Note: Rubbing alcohol works very well for cleaning ink, but eventually it will rust your letters if they are not dried off properly, so make sure you do.*

The green ink will wear off in a couple days, after he smears it all over his face and everyone else in the herd!

A word of caution: If you do happen to nick a vein when you are tattooing (as I did this morning on Asteroid's brother, Alfalfa) stay calm and don't panic. Apply pressure to the bleed and liberally apply blood stop powder ASAP, and the bleeding will stop. This was the first time I've ever nicked a vein when tattooing. I was prepared, and the blood stop powder was only about 5 feet away. It bled ALOT, but I managed to get it stopped quickly and he is no worse for the wear.

UDDERS AND MILKING

The udder is an amazing structure. If you are at all interested in milking your goats, you should first understand some basic anatomical terms concerning the udder of the milking goat.

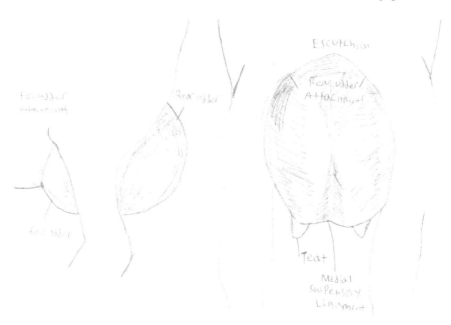

There are many attachments which hold the udder to the body of the goat and provide structure to the udder. The main areas of attachments are the rear udder attachments, the fore udder attachments, lateral attachments (attachments which hold the udder to the inside of the thighs), and the medial suspensory ligament (MSL) which divides the udder halves and holds the udder floor up. The udder halves are not connected and act independently of each other.

Internal Mammary Structure

The alveoli, which are sack-like microstructures, is the place where milk is produced. Hundreds of alveoli are clustered together to form a lobule. Many lobules make up a lobe. Each lobe, structured like a small cluster of grapes, have a complex duct system that moves the milk from the lobes down to the gland cistern where the bulk of the milk is stored. If the gland cistern is full, there are also minor cisterns near major lobes, where the milk is stored intermediately as it moves toward the gland cistern. Milk is also stored in the duct systems of the udder. The gland cistern is the last stop for the milk, right before it is expressed from the orifice of a teat.

Some additional thoughts: Udders fill from the bottom up, first the gland cistern is filled, and then minor cisterns situated close to lobes will fill. Milk is produced on a supply/demand system. If you want more milk then milk more often. If you want less milk, then milk less often. The goat, if she is being properly fed, will adjust.

So you might be asking yourself...why does it even matter if I know how an udder works? Let's learn about milking, and I think you will understand.

How to Hand Milk a Goat

For this section, I am using much of my original 01/06/2013 blog post from my farm page. A link to the original post is on the website at **www.thegoatchick.com**

Supplies
- A goat in milk
- A stanchion w/ feeder
- A milk stool
- Some grain and/or alfalfa pellets
- Paper towels & 10% Bleach water solution in a spray bottle OR Unscented Baby Wipes OR Teat Wipes
- 1 clean & sanitized milk bucket
- Fight-Bac Teat Disinfectant Spray

How to milk:

First, lead the doe to the stanchion. Ours usually come out of the stall willingly and go to the stanchion on their own, and when we have more than one doe milking they will come to the gate to be milked, in the same order, every day. Feed your doe grain in the stanchion so that she is occupied during milking. This creates a pleasant experience for the doe and is enough to make her want to come to the parlor to be milked the next time.

Cleanliness before, during, and after milking is paramount, especially if you intend to consume the milk, which we do. Clean the teats and udder with baby wipes, or bleach solution and paper towels.

I prefer to milk from behind the doe, but you can easily milk from the side as well. If the doe is used to being milked and is content with letting you milk her while she eats, I find that milking both teats from behind is the easiest and fastest way to get it done. Place the bucket in front of and centered between the doe's back legs, underneath but slightly forward of the teats. Now you are ready to milk.

Milk is let down when oxytocin is produced. Bump and massage the udder a couple of times to get the oxytocin flowing to trigger the letdown of milk. The trick to milking is to trap the milk at the base of the teat with your fingers and roll it out of the teat with your other fingers. I like to use my thumb and index finger in a circle to trap the milk, and then gently close each of my other fingers in turn to gently extract the milk out of the orifice. When the teat is empty, I release my thumb and forefinger to let more milk into the teat, trap it again with my thumb and forefinger, and repeat the extraction by closing my other fingers down the length of the teat. Sometimes, I milk both teats simultaneously, while other times I alternate one teat and then the other. Whichever way you decide, it is important to milk both sides evenly to keep the two halves of the udder producing equal amounts of milk.

The key to milking is to be gentle, yet firm and always be calm. Milking should be a relaxing experience for the goat as well as for the milker. Never pull or otherwise displace the natural position of the udder or teats.

You should be able to gauge whether or not your doe is relaxed. If she tenses (and this is easy to gauge if you are paying attention) she may kick over or step in the bucket, so you need to be quick in the calmest way, and remove the bucket from under her before she moves. This tension or restlessness in the doe usually means that her grain is gone, and she wants more. When this happens, I remove the bucket and set it in a safe place, refill the grain, and start again. If she does kick over the bucket before you remove it, do not worry. It happens!! Clean it up and start over again. I've spilled lots of milk and had lots of hooves in the milk bucket!

When you think the doe is near empty, massage the upper part of the udder to trigger those higher lobes and cisterns to let more milk down into the gland cistern. This is called the "hind milk" and many inexperienced breeders miss it. Remember, that milk is supplied according to demand, so if you miss this hind milk, it might not be there tomorrow.

To finish milking, remove the bucket from the stand. Spray each teat with FightBac teat spray or a similar teat dip to seal out bacteria that would enter the teat. Release your doe from the stanchion.

Handling Milk

- Milk should be filtered before you store it, as in...as quickly as possible. Even if you can't see it, there are bound to be little hairs and specks of dust that settled in the milk while you were milking. We use a small piece of butter muslin (fine cheesecloth) and pour the collected milk directly into a Ball jar or milk jug. You can also buy milk filters and milk screens that go over the top of your bucket to filter out impurities as you milk.
- Milk should be cooled as rapidly as possible to preserve flavor and freshness. To cool it quickly, put your bucket into an ice bath and get it down <40° F rapidly.
- Glass jars are best for storing milk. The glass will keep the milk fresher longer. Plastic milk jugs work too, as long as they are cleaned and sterilized before using them. Plastic is porous and therefore can release unwanted flavors into your delicious milk.
- If you choose to pasteurize your milk before using it, you can use an automatic pasteurizer, or you can heat your milk in a pot to 161°F for 15 seconds, and then cool it in an ice bath.
- Raw goats milk doesn't really "spoil" it just turns into something else. If you leave your milk in the refrigerator too long, it will likely turn into a sour cream like concoction called clabber, which you can actually use for a ton of things. Pasteurized milk WILL SPOIL.
- Cream does not readily rise to the top of goat's milk, as it is naturally homogenized. If you leave a jar of goat's milk undisturbed for 3-5 days you'll be able to collect a bit of heavy cream off the top.
- Raw goats milk will stay fresh for 10-14 days or longer, depending on how it was handled from the beginning.

Milking Machines

There are dozens of electric and hand actuated milking machines on the market. Most are expensive, require regular maintenance, and require daily cleaning and sanitizing. I cannot recommend any current models, but there are many message boards and groups that you can join to get opinions on all of the options. Even when I am milking 10+ does, I find milking machines to be cumbersome, so I no longer personally use them, although I totally understand why many people do.

What Can I Do With All This Extra Milk?
- Make Cheese
- Make Yogurt
- Make Kefir
- Make Ice Cream
- Make Lotion
- Make Soap and MORE!

I recommend the New England Cheesemaking Company for cheese, yogurt and kefir recipes and supplies, and The Soap Queen for lotions and soap recipes. You can find cosmetic ingredients and packaging at Brambleberry and Bulk Apothecary. Have fun!

PERFORMANCE PROGRAMS
This section is specifically geared towards dairy goats.

DHIR (Milk Testing)
DHIR (Dairy Herd Improvement Registry) is a program that tests the quantity and quality of milk regularly produced by a specific doe. The program also collects genetic data. Sires can also win awards based on the production data of daughters. Registries like the American Dairy Goat Association (ADGA) and the American Goat Society (AGS) have specific requirements to participate and to win awards based on production. For specific requirements visit ADGA or AGS.

Linear Appraisal & AGS Classification
Both ADGA and AGS have a system for scoring a doe or buck against the ideal breed standards. In each, an appraiser comes to evaluate each animal in your herd and apply a scorecard to the animal to come up with a number which represents the percentage points an animal earns when scored against the ideal dairy goat. A perfect score is 100, which has never and will never happen, because there is no such thing as a perfect goat. Visit ADGA to learn about Linear Appraisals and visit AGS to learn more about AGS Classification programs.

DNA & Typing
The DNA typing service is a permanent record of identification of individual animals. Collection of hair follicles creates a DNA record of a specific animal. For some breeds, there are typing programs such as G-6-S and Alpha S-1 Casein typing, which can provide information that may be important to your breeding program with regards to milk and cheesemaking properties.

ADGA Genetics

ADGA provides a website where you can see all the accumulated data on animals, try out breedings (on paper) to see how breeding might go based on accumulated data, and access USDA and production records of registered animals. You can look up any ADGA registered animal at www.adgagenetics.org

UNDERSTANDING PEDIGREES

Pedigrees can be pretty intimidating, so I'm going to break it down for you. For this exercise, I've pulled a four-generation pedigree on my doe, Honey, on ADGA Subscription Reports and I marked it up to show the relationships of ancestors to her.

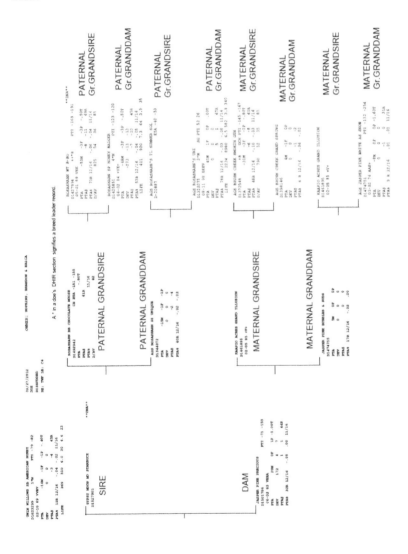

The graphic on the previous page is a goat's family tree. In the first generation, it shows Honey's Dam and Sire and any relevant production data collected on them. The next row, in the middle, shows Honey's Dam and Sire's Parents and any relevant production data collected on them. In the last row, four generations back, it shows Honey's Great Grandparents and any relevant production data collected on them.
So, what does all of this mean? Let's focus on Honey's data first, which you will find in the upper left corner of the pedigree.

```
TWIN WILLOWS SB AMERICAN HONEY                    09/27/2012
D1623299        1*M        PTI -70 -82            DOE
  03-10 89 VVEV                                   DISBUDDED
PTA           -16M    -1F    -1P  -.40T           RE: TWF LE: C4
DEV             0      0      0
PTA$                  -3     -4       43R
PTA%  19R 12/16     -.04   -.02    11/16
  LIFE          269   500   6.0   30   4.6   23
```

First, you will see her registered name, Twin Willows SB American Honey. Twin Willows is the herd name. "SB" stands for Starbuck, which is her sire's name. Many farms attach a sire designator between the herd name and her actual name, which in this case is American Honey. To the left of her name, you will find her date of birth, the fact that she is a doe, that she is disbudded, and then under that you will find her tattoos, which are unique from every other goat registered in ADGA. In case you missed the explanation of tattoos, she has TWF tattooed in her right ear, and C4 tattooed in her right ear. The right ear (TWF) shows the unique herd tattoo sequence, and the left ear (C4) shows that she was born in 2012 (C) and she was the 4th baby born that year at Twin Willows.

Under her name you will see D1623299. The "D" stands for Nigerian Dwarf. All Nigis registered with ADGA start with a D, and then the string of numbers is assigned by ADGA based on when she was registered. This is Honey's official ADGA registration number.

To the right of her registration number, you will see 1*M. This means that she is a first-generation breed leader for milk. If her dam was starred, then this number would say 2*M, and her dam would be 1*M, and so on. Any daughters born to Honey who earn their Milk Stars will be 2*M. Stars are earned by having high milk volume, butterfat and/or protein content in her milk.

Next, we are going to jump down to the last line and you will find her milking stats. Next to LIFE, which stands for Lifetime Total you will find some numbers. The first number 269 designates the period of time she was milk tested, 269 days. The next number, 500, means that she milked 500 pounds of milk in that 269 days. The next two numbers, 6.0 & 30, means that she averaged 6% butterfat in that 269 days, and in that period of time, she milked 30 pounds of butterfat. The final two numbers, 4.6 and 23, means that in 269 days she averaged 4.6% protein and in total she milked 23 pounds of protein.

Now, as a side note: The amounts of milk, butterfat and protein that you have to milk in order to earn a milk star is based on the age of the doe at the time she freshened. She starred when she was a first freshener, and she was fourteen months old when she freshened. In order for her to star, she needed to milk at least 600# of milk, 21# of butterfat, and 18# of protein. In her case, she officially starred in butterfat and protein as a first freshener in ADGA. AGS has different requirements. You can find star requirements on both the ADGA website and the AGS website.

www.adga.org
www.americangoatsociety.com

Now, we are going to jump back up to right underneath Honey's registration number, where you will see some numbers and letters starting with 03-10. This indicated that Honey was last appraised when she was 3 years and 10 months old. And next to that, you will see the results of that appraisal. Her final score was an 89, which is 89% of ideal, and in the Very Good category (one point away from Excellent, darnit! Maybe next year.)

Excellent (E)   90-100
Very Good(V)   85-89
Good Plus (+)   80-84
Acceptable (A) 70-79
Fair (F)   60-69
Poor   <60

To the right of the final score you will see four letters VVEV. The first letter (V) is for General Appearance. Honey appraised as Very Good in that category. The second letter (V) is for Dairy Strength. Honey appraised as Very Good in that category. The third letter (E) is for Body Capacity. Honey appraised as Excellent in that category. The last letter (V) is for Mammary. Honey appraised as Very Good in that category. If you scroll back up, you will see some Linear Appraisals that were conducted on some of Honey's ancestors, including some bucks. Bucks can be appraised too, but they are only scored on the first three categories, because they do not have Mammaries. :)

Ok...now for the hard stuff...

Of those letters and numbers that are left around Honey's name that we have not yet discussed, these are the most difficult to understand. Let's break it down.

PTA

PTA stands for Predicted Transmitting Ability. These numbers are calculated based on the animal's data and the data of her ancestors and progeny for both production and type. The first three numbers predict the pounds of milk, butterfat and protein from each lactation of the animal's future daughters when compared to a herd mate of average genetic merit. The last number is the PTA of change to the Type score. These numbers rank animals based on genetic merit.

DEV

This is the Standard Deviation we can expect in pounds.

PTA$

These numbers stand for Predicted Transmitting Ability Dollars. It is an economic index that estimates the extra dollars that a breeder would receive in each lactation based on the data provided. The first number stands for fat, the second for protein and the third number, is percentage confidence that these numbers are accurate.

PTA%

Predicted Transmitting Ability Percentage.
Reliability score for Production, first score is Fat, second score is Protein. First date is last date production was calculated and the last date is when type was calculated.

PTI

PTI stands for Production Type Indexes--this is a genetic index that takes into account all of the above data and combines production and genetic evaluations into one score. The first number emphasizes production. The second number emphasizes type. Zero=no change.

Other Designations on Dairy Pedigrees

	ADGA	AGS
Champion- Animal won 3 official championships under at least 2 judges.	CH	MCH
Permanent Grand Champion- A goat than has achieved Champion status and also has earned a milk star.	GCH	ARMCH
Advanced Registry- Doe earned her milk star through DHIR programs.	AR	AR
Star Volume- Doe earned her milk star on one day test or owner sampler program or on the basis of pedigree or progeny.	ST	ST
Star Doe- A doe that meets the minimum requirements for milk production OR has 3 star daughters, or two star sons, or 2 star daughters and one star son.	*M	*D
Star Sire- A buck that has a starred dam and has a starred sire with a starred dam.	*B	*S
Plus Sire- A buck that has at least 3 starred daughters from different does, or has 2 starred sons, or has 2 starred daughters and 1 starred son.	+B	+S
Two Plus Sire- A buck that has at least 3 starred daughters from different does and at least 2 starred sons.	++B	++S
Two Plus Star Sire- A buck that has at least 3 starred daughters, 2 starred sons, and a starred dam or sire.	++*B	++*S
Superior Genetics- A doe or a buck that is in the top 15% of the production index for that breed.	SG	----
Superior Genetics Permanent Grand Champion- A doe or a buck who has earned both SG designation and Permanent Grand Champion Status	SGCH	----
ELITE- If ELITE follows PTA$, the animal is in the top 15% of its breed for Milk Fat Protein Dollars.	ELITE	----
Daughter Averages- D(aughter) AV(erages) Milk, Fat, Protein, Final Score	D/AV	----
DNA- DNA is on file for this animal at the registry.	**DNA**	----
AGS- AGS pedigree used to register with ADGA.	AGS	----

BLUE EYED AND POLLED GENETICS

Blue Eyed Genetics

Blue eyes are found most commonly in Nigerian Dwarfs or Nigerian Dwarf crosses. Blue eyes are dominant in goats, so if one parent has blue eyes, then there is a good chance that he can produce blue-eyed babies. Let's explore the genetics of blue eyed goats. As you know, each goat has two parents, a dam and a sire. For these examples, a brown eyed gene will be identified as **b**, and a blue-eyed gene will be identified as **B**.

First, a little explanation of terms:

Each parent gives ONE gene for eye color to each kid, either a brown gene (b) or a blue gene (B).

Heterozygous- A goat that has blue eyes, but she inherited one b gene and one B gene from her parents.
Homozygous- A goat has blue eyes, and she inherited a B gene from both of her parents, who were also both blue eyed.

Since blue eyes are a dominant trait, if a goat has BROWN EYES, then you can assume that the goat has bb eye color genetics. If a goat has blue eyes, then they can be heterozygous for blue eyes (Bb) or homozygous for blue eyes (BB) based upon which genes they received from their parents.

For our first example, let's say that you have a doe who is brown eyed (bb), and she is crossed with a buck who is heterozygous for blue eyes (Bb). When we apply these genes to a grid, you can quickly see the results.

	b	b
B	Bb	Bb
b	bb	bb

In the above case, a brown eyed doe is bred with a buck who is heterozygous for blue eyes. In two cases, the baby with end up with brown eyes, and in two cases the baby ends up with blue eyes. This does not mean that 50% of the babies will have brown eyes, and 50% of the babies will have blue eyes. It means that EACH BABY has a 50% chance of having blue eyes in this case and they will all be heterozygous (Bb) for blue eyes.

Now, let's breed a heterozygous doe, with a homozygous buck.

	b	B
B	Bb	BB
B	Bb	BB

In the above case, all babies will be blue eyed, but EACH BABY has a 50% chance of being homozygous (BB) and EACH BABY has a 50% chance of being heterozygous (Bb) for blue eyes.

In the final case, we will breed a heterozygous (Bb) doe with a heterozygous (Bb) buck.

	B	b
B	BB	Bb
b	Bb	bb

You will notice that this case, the breedings result in heterozygous blue at a rate of 50%, homozygous blue at a rate of 25% and brown eyed babies at a rate of 25%. Again, this DOES NOT MEAN that 75% of the babies born will have blue eyes, it means that EACH baby has a 75% chance of having blue eyes. In a litter from this example, you could have 100% blue eyed babies, or 100% brown eyed babies.

Polled Genetics
Polled means naturally hornless. The genetic example of polled vs. horned goats works very similarly to the blue-eyed vs brown eyes example above. The polled gene, like the blue-eyed gene, is dominant in goats. We will use the P to represent a polled gene, and an h to represent a horned gene. Again, each parent gives ONE GENE to each kid. Just like the blue-eyed genetics, here are also heterozygous (**Ph**) and homozygous (**PP**) horn genetics.

WARNING: It has been shown through research, that breeding a polled doe to a polled buck which results in a PP (Polled X Polled) genetic marker will result in the kid having a higher incidence of intersex or hermaphroditic characteristics. For the purpose of these genetic exercises, we will show the results of these breedings, but it is not recommended.

For the first example, let's breed a heterozygous doe to a horned buck.

	P	h
h	Ph	hh
h	Ph	hh

In the above case, each kid has a 50% chance of being polled, and a 50% chance of being horned, with NO INCIDENCE of homozygous polled genetics.

Now let's breed a horned doe with a homozygous buck.

	h	h
P	Ph	Ph
P	Ph	Ph

Because polled genes are dominant, all kids will be polled, but none of them will be homozygous for polled genetics.

Finally, let's breed a homozygous doe with a homozygous buck.

	P	P
P	PP	PP
P	PP	PP

In the final case above, all kids will be polled and homozygous for polled genetics.

AFTERWORD

Deciding to move to the country to raise goats has been one of the most important decisions of my life. After seven years of raising these wonderful little creatures, I truly cannot imagine a life without my goats. But, raising goats is not for everyone and the learning curve is steep. I have attempted to compile this information as a basic guide of what I have learned over the years. I'm still learning. In fact, I learn something new every single day as new situations arise, so there will, no doubt, be further editions with updated information in the future.

Send your goat related questions to **erica@thegoatchick.com** to receive a personalized response, and a chance to have your question featured in future editions of this book.

I hope that this book has helped you decide whether or not you would like to raise goats, and I wish you luck in your goat endeavors. If you are ever passing through Central Indiana, be sure to look me up and stop by for a visit. I would love to show you around, introduce you to my herd, and "talk goats."

Best Regards,

Erica, The Goat Chick
erica@thegoatchick.com

www.thegoatchick.com
www.twinwillowsfarm.net

Like my farm on Facebook!
facebook.com/twinwillowsnigerians

Made in the USA
Monee, IL
15 February 2022